The SECRET LIVES of MEN

A WOMEN'S GUIDE TO MALE DECEPTION, OMISSION & SILENCE

MINA V. ADLER

MINERVA DOY
PUBLISHING

Paperback ISBN: 978-1-7646319-6-9

Hardcover ISBN: 978-1-7646319-7-6

Ebook ISBN: 978-1-7646319-8-3

For my spiritual progenitors –
my great grandmother, Elizabeth Lee
and my grandmother, Sybil Geraldine
– with love and gratitude.

About the Author

Mina V. Adler

Mina V. Adler writes with fury, wit, and zero tolerance for male secrecy.

A student of human behaviour and a lifelong feminist (and not a misandrist), Ms Adler exposes the hidden rooms men keep from women—sometimes harmless, often damaging—and refuses to soften the truth for anyone's comfort.

She blends humorous disdain with piercing insight, chronicling the quiet manipulations, omissions, and secrets men cultivate. She believes women deserve clarity, truth, and the freedom to stop doing the emotional labour men are trained to outsource.

Ms Adler drinks strong coffee, eviscerates patriarchal norms for breakfast, reads everything that challenges conventional thinking, and believes laughter is the sharpest tool women have in a world built to excuse men.

Mina V. Adler 2026

Photo credit: Abe Blue

The Secret Lives of Men

A Women's Guide to Male Deception, Omission & Silence

Mina V. Adler

Contents

INTRODUCTION

A Modern Fable of Secrecy

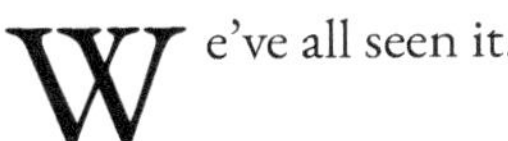

e've all seen it.

The meme with a single On/Off switch labeled *Men.*

And a sprawling, incomprehensible tangle of dials, levers, and blinking lights labeled *Women*.

Supposedly funny, supposedly confirming what society tells us every day: women are complicated, men are simple.

Let me tell you the truth: *men are the complicated ones.*

That single switch? An illusion. The real machine—the hidden wiring—is a labyrinth of secrets, shame vaults, avoidance levers, ego regulators, and emotional bypass circuits.

Every flick of a hidden switch is a past they refuse to admit, a desire they dare not speak, or a habit they've been trained to conceal.

The blinking lights? Guilt, confusion, jealousy, resentment—all strobing beneath the calm surface they present to the world.

And who is expected to navigate this maze?

You.

Women.

With no manual, no warning signs, and no training, we're expected to interpret moods, decode silences, and translate evasions into explanations that maintain harmony—because heaven forbid a man should confront his own discomfort.

The irony is delicious: women are "complicated" because *we must be.* We have to be. Every adjustment of tone, patience, and strategy is survival: keeping a relationship functioning while men remain blissfully unexamined, shielded from accountability, and emotionally understocked.

Men look simple because society has outsourced the difficult work of honesty, self-reflection, and emotional labor onto women.

The meme lies.

The complexity isn't ours. It's theirs—and we've been living it for them for far too long.

The next time someone laughs at that meme, remember: the joke is decades old, and the punchline is that women are still sorting out wiring behind it.

The truth is revolutionary: men are trained to be complicated, and women are trained to tolerate it.

The most remarkable and confusing complication?

Men's penchant for secrecy.

Let's be honest: Men have secrets. All of them.

Even the "decent" ones. Even the gentle ones. Even the ones who say they "hate drama."

If anything, the self-proclaimed "good men" are often the most practised at concealing—the most polished, the most curated, the most quietly evasive.

Not necessarily dangerous. Not necessarily malicious. But strategic.

Because men grow up learning one core lesson: If you keep quiet, women will fill in the blanks in your favour.

And they do.

Women smooth the edges. Women rationalise the behaviour. Women swallow the questions. Women trust because society punishes them when they don't.

Male secrecy isn't an accident; it's a system. A privilege. A luxury men were handed at birth.

What This Book Is (And What It Isn't)
This is not a book about undermining or hating men.

It's a book about *finally seeing them clearly*—without the soft focus, without the excuses, without the social pressure to be endlessly understanding while receiving scraps of emotional truth in return.

It's a book about:

- **the kinds of secrets men keep (and why).**

- **the emotional shortcuts they rely on.**

- **the silent expectations placed on women to "manage" it.**

- **the ways women are discouraged from trusting their own perception.**

- **the cultural machinery that trains men to hide and women to tolerate.**

It's a book about patterns, not paranoia.

Because the issue is not that men have secrets. Human beings have secrets. The issue is how comfortably men are allowed to keep theirs—and how uncomfortably women are forced to live around them.

Women Aren't Crazy—Men *Are* Hiding Things
And we're tired of pretending otherwise.

Every woman knows the feeling: that tiny tug in the gut when something about a man doesn't add up.

A paused breath. A story that's a little too tidy. A detail that feels airbrushed. A mood you can't quite decode. A silence that stretches longer than it should.

And every woman has been told—repeatedly, patronisingly—to ignore it.

"Don't be paranoid."

"Don't be dramatic."

"He's a good guy."

"You're overthinking."

"Men just aren't emotional like that."

Translation: *Doubt your instincts. Protect his comfort. Silence yourself so he never has to speak.*

This book exists because women are exhausted.

Exhausted from carrying the emotional load.

Exhausted from decoding men.

Exhausted from performing psychological gymnastics just to maintain "peace."

Exhausted from being told that wanting clarity is "too demanding."

You Are Not Imagining It

That flicker of suspicion? It's not neurosis.

That moment of "something's off"? It's not insecurity.

That sense he's withholding? It's not overreaction.

Women have been gaslit for generations into believing their intuition is a defect. Meanwhile, men have been socially rewarded for selective honesty, emotional retreat, and well-timed vagueness.

This book dismantles the idea that male secrecy is normal, harmless, or acceptable.

Because secrecy is rarely benign.

It creates imbalance. It creates confusion. It forces women into detective work they never volunteered for.

And most of all—it trains women to shrink themselves in the name of "understanding him."

A New Framework: Not How to Fix Men, But How to Stop Fixing What Men Hide

You're not here to learn how to coax confessions or "communicate better" or gently guide a man into emotional adulthood. Women have been doing that unpaid labor for centuries.

This book will give you:

- **language for the evasions you've always sensed**

- **clarity around the types of secrets men cling to**

- **tools to stop absorbing the consequences of male avoidance**

- **permission to stop tolerating what drains you**

- **a map of men's inner compartments—so you can see the patterns without getting trapped in them.**

This is not a guide to make men talk. It's a guide to stop letting men's silence undo you.

The Revolution Starts With Seeing

Men are not mysteries. They are simply accustomed to living unexamined lives while expecting women to accommodate whatever truth they refuse to face.

But once you see the system, you can't un-see it.

Once you name the pattern, you can't fall for it again.

Once you recognise what men hide and why, you step out of confusion and into clarity.

And clarity is freedom.

This book isn't here to make you suspicious. It's here to make you *impossible to gaslight.*

Let's get started. Let's open the doors they never expected women to stop knocking on. Not to expose, but to understand.

Let's talk about the quiet secrets—the ones hiding behind the word *good.*

Ready?

Good.

Because men have had centuries of being protected.

It's time women stop paying the price for their silence.

PART 1 – WHY MEN HIDE

Chapter 1

A Taxonomy of Male Secrets

A Field Guide to the Hidden Corners of His Life

Let's dive right in with a truth so obvious it has somehow become invisible: men have entire ecosystems of secrets, carefully maintained like little bonsai forests of shame and convenience.

Men don't just keep secrets.

They curate them.

They alphabetize them.

They build entire underground vaults of emotional contraband.

Women are expected to politely pretend they don't see any of it. And when they do, they are blamed for finding out.

Men act astonished — *astonished!* — when a woman stumbles across something she was "never meant to see."

Men's secrecy is not a glitch in the system.

It *is* the system.

It's the oxygen so many relationships secretly run on.

We've been trained — socially, romantically, generationally — to accept the quiet hum of male secrecy the same way we accept power lines buzzing overhead. We know it's there, we know it's not great for us, and yet we carry on because we've been told it's "normal."

But here's the thing: *It isn't normal.*

And it isn't harmless.

In fact, once you start naming the kinds of secrets men carry, a pattern emerges — a taxonomy, almost biological in its precision. Because when you sort male secrets into categories, you can finally see the structure of the behaviour that for decades has been mislabelled as "boys will be boys," "men are just private," or the deepest insult of all: "You're overreacting."

No. You're not overreacting.

You've simply never been handed the field guide.

Men market themselves as the emotionally uncomplicated sex — the "straightforward" ones who "say what they mean" — while women are supposedly the labyrinthine mysteries of the species. And yet, once you actually start digging, you'll find that men contain more hidden compartments than a 19th-century pirate chest.

Women aren't the confusing ones; we're the *transparent* ones. We overshare. We narrate our inner worlds. We confide. We ask. We check in. We explain.

Meanwhile, men maintain a private inner server room full of blinking red lights, sealed doors, encrypted drives, and long, unchanging passwords — and half the time *they've forgotten their own login.*

This book doesn't claim that all men are villains, cheaters, or abusers. But it does claim — unapologetically — that even the "good ones" keep secrets, and those secrets shape the emotional landscape of women's lives. Sometimes dramatically. Sometimes subtly. Always silently.

So let's map the terrain.

Let's name the creatures.

Let's catalogue the whole damn species.

Behold, the **Taxonomy of Male Secrets** – the comprehensive field guide for any woman who's ever had the creeping suspicion that something wasn't quite right, but doubted herself instead of the man standing in front of her.

It's part anthropology, part forensic evidence — of what men hide, why they hide it, and the collateral damage women are left to sort through.

The point of this taxonomy is simple: to show women that male secrecy is not random.

It is patterned. Predictable. Cultural. And it lands entirely on *our* bodies, *our* lives, and *our* emotional labor.

CATEGORY 1: The Shame-Based Secrets
"If I never say it out loud, it isn't real."

These are the secrets men bury because they fear judgment — not legal judgment, not moral judgment, but *female* judgment. Their mother's judgment, their partner's judgment, the imaginary tribunal of Women Who Expect Better.

These include:
Their porn habits.
Their insecurities.
Their failures.
Their emotional needs.

Anything that would make them appear fragile, mortal, or — god forbid — human.

These secrets are the silent killers of intimacy. While women share vulnerability to *build* closeness, men often hide vulnerability to *maintain* power or dignity.

And who pays the cost? Women, who are forced to intuit what is wrong without ever being given the information required to fix it.

The ripple effect is enormous: emotional labor, confusion, self-doubt, blame, and the sense of being shut out of a relationship you're supposed to be half of.

CATEGORY 2: The Convenience Secrets

"I didn't tell you because it was easier not to."

Ah yes — the secrets that don't come from fear but from laziness. These are the omissions, the "forgot to mentions," the little details that would have created conversation, accountability, or consequence.

Examples:
The money spent.

The messages exchanged.

The work wife.

The drink after work.

The flirtations when you're not present, or even when you are.

The woman he used to sleep with who is now "just a friend".

The plan he made without you.

The bill he hid.

The thing he broke.

These are the secrets that cause women to ask, "Why didn't you just tell me?"

And men to respond, "I dunno, I didn't think it mattered," or the even more insulting, "I didn't want to deal with a reaction."

Let's translate: *He wanted to avoid consequences, so he outsourced the fallout to you.*

Convenience secrecy creates resentment, inequality, and the subtle realisation that you are the "manager" of the relationship, while he gets to be the "employee" who selectively reports up — or doesn't.

CATEGORY 3: The Habitual Secrets

"This is just how I am."

Some men are lifelong secret-keepers — taught from boyhood to conceal, compartmentalise, and cover up. These men aren't necessarily hiding big-ticket betrayals. Instead, they hide *anything* that feels personal.

To them, privacy isn't a boundary; it's a reflex.

These men:

Hide emotions.
Hide thoughts.
Hide discomfort.
Hide desire.
Hide fears.
Hide dissatisfaction.
Hide exhaustion.

And because they're so used to hiding, they often genuinely believe they *aren't* lying — that silence isn't deception, just "being low-key." Meanwhile, their partners exist in a perpetual guessing game.

Women in relationships with these men often describe the same sensation: It is like living with someone who is physically present but emotionally ghostlike.

The cost is a chronic sense of distance.

A loneliness you cannot name because technically you are not alone.

CATEGORY 4: The Ego-Protecting Secrets
"I'll tell you the version that makes me look good."

Ah, the classics.

These are not lies — not outright fabrications — but curated omissions designed to preserve a man's sense of self as the capable, moral, admirable version he prefers you see.

These include:
Sanitised stories from his past.
Downplayed mistakes.

Minimised conflicts.
Omitted flirtations.
Misrepresented intentions.
Rewritten history.

This is the signature secrecy of the "good man." The man who prides himself on not being like other men.

But the truth is: *Even good men edit themselves for women.*

Some do it to keep the peace.

Some do it to maintain hero status.

Some do it because they want the benefits of intimacy without the vulnerability that earns it.

The impact on partners?

A gradual erosion of trust combined with the slow, unsettling realisation that you have fallen in love with a curated persona, not a full human being.

CATEGORY 5: The Male-Culture Secrets
"I'd never tell you the things I tell my mates."

If women knew even 20% of the conversations that men have in all-male spaces, civilisation would have collapsed decades ago.

These secrets include:
The downplaying of partners' accomplishments.
The resentment of domestic labor.

The emotional disclosures given to friends but withheld from partners.

The bravado about porn, exes, bodies, conquests.

The sexual jokes.

The offhand, disparaging, disrespectful remarks about women that are deemed "normal male humor" or "harmless locker room talk".

These secrets matter because they reveal the *double life* many women sense but cannot pinpoint: the man he is with you versus the man he is in the pack.

The cost to women: The jarring feeling that you know him — but you also... don't.

Not fully.

Not the version he shows his male peers.

CATEGORY 6: The Hidden-Until-Too-Late Secrets

Where he insists "it wasn't relevant" but, mysteriously, it absolutely was.

These are the secrets that are "in the past" (according to him) but *directly shape the present* (according to reality).

i) The Ex Files

What he doesn't tell you:

The ex he "barely remembers" once lived with him.

The "friend from uni" is actually an ex he tried to get back with three times.

The reason they broke up was... well, complicated (read: his fault).

Impact on women: You walk into social situations unarmed. Someone mentions her name. Everyone else tenses. He changes the subject. And you're the one who feels embarrassed or humiliated.

ii) The Children He Wasn't Going to Mention Yet

Yes. This happens. More than you think.

There are men who wait months — sometimes years — before revealing the existence of offspring.

Their reasoning? "It didn't feel like the right time."

Translation: *He knew it would change how you saw him.*

iii) The Secret Long-Term Relationship

Not quite an ex, not quite current. But still very much in the background — texting, signing off with kisses, orbiting, occasionally "meeting up for a drink".

CATEGORY 7: The Emotional Black-Hole Secrets

The secrets that have shaped him — but for which he provides no user manual.

Men insist they are simple.

They are not. They are fortresses with childhood trauma buried under the floorboards.

i) The Inability to Feel (Which He Thinks Is Normal)

He doesn't tell you he hasn't cried since 2003.

He doesn't tell you his father only spoke in criticism.

He doesn't tell you his mother's love was conditional.

Instead, he tells you: "I'm just not emotional."

Women then spend entire relationships trying to decode behaviour that would have made perfect sense if he'd simply admitted:

"My emotional development stalled at ten."

ii) The Anger He Pretends He Doesn't Have

Rage at work.

Rage on the road.

Rage at minor inconveniences.

You only ever see a teaspoonful of what's beneath the surface, because he is *terrified* that if he opens the lid even a crack, he'll incinerate the room.

iii) The Shame Files

Every man has one: a secret folder of insecurities he will never name.

So he hides it through:

Deflection.

Withdrawal.

Sarcasm.

Or sudden, disproportionate irritation.

Women feel the effects.

Men pretend nothing happened.

CATEGORY 8: The Behavioural Secrets

Things he does that he hopes you never find out.

i) The Financial Shadow Life

Not necessarily malicious — but always impactful.

Examples:

Hidden debt.

Secret bank accounts or credit cards.

Gambling, ranging from "just now and then" to "we're losing the house".

The crypto account that tanked months ago.

The savings account he started without telling you "because it's mine".

Women don't find out until something breaks: the budget, the trust, or both.

ii) The Porn Habits He Pretends Are Normal

Not "man watches porn" — that's hardly a novelty. It's the sneakiness that hurts. The *secretiveness.*

Hidden accounts.
Deleted histories.
Kinks he thinks you'd "judge".
Hours spent scrolling instead of being present.

And the inevitable fallout: You think you're the problem.

You think your libido is mismatched.

You think he's no longer attracted to you.

When the truth is: he kept you in the dark about what was actually happening.

iii) The Emotional Affairs He Doesn't Acknowledge

Men think an affair only counts if there's penetration.

Women know the real betrayal usually begins long before that.

Cue:
The "old friend" or work wife he texts at midnight and includes kisses.
The online DMs and social media comments that "don't mean anything".

If you found the messages, you wouldn't call it innocent. You'd be blamed for looking at his phone, even if it proves your suspicions.

He calls it "nothing to worry about." He deflects.

Suddenly you're the guilty party.

CATEGORY 9: The Secrets That Become Your Burden

Where his lack of disclosure becomes your emotional labor.

i) The Mental Health He Won't Name

He won't admit he's depressed.
He won't admit he's anxious.
He won't admit he's burnt out.

He just becomes harder to live with.

You start adapting. You start compensating.

You start doing the emotional heavy lifting that he refuses to acknowledge.

ii) The Insecurities He Projects Onto You

When he feels inadequate, somehow *you* become "difficult," "demanding," "overly sensitive," or "expecting too much."

His secrecy becomes your "attitude problem."

iii) The Past Mistakes He Hopes Never Surface

Deep down, he believes you wouldn't love him if you knew the whole truth.

So he withholds the whole truth.

And then acts like you're unreasonable for wanting a partner you can actually *know*.

CATEGORY 10: The Big Betrayal Secrets
"This one would change EVERYTHING if you knew."

These secrets sit at the bottom of the ocean—the deepest, darkest, most pressurised zone of the taxonomy.

These include:
Emotional affairs.
Physical affairs.
Secret children.
Secret debts.
Drug or alcohol addictions.
Hidden porn addictions.

The massage parlor visits:
"It was just a massage."
"OK it was a hand-job."
"OK but it only happened once."
"OK I paid a sex worker for sex."
"OK but it only happened once."
"I was just curious."
"It's your fault for ignoring my needs/withholding."
"Men have neeeeeds!"

And when all else fails, "You snooped at my phone. You invaded my privacy. You're the one who can't be trusted!"

Secret double lives and hidden criminal behaviour– the dark web, the crimes, the exploitation.

The kind of thing that, once uncovered, rewrites the entire story of your relationship.

The kind of secret that detonates.

Women do not blame themselves for these secrets — not consciously.

But they often feel the secondary wound: shame for not seeing it sooner. Shame for trusting. Shame for believing the relationship was safe.

This category, more than any other, highlights the central thesis of this book: *Male secrecy is not a personality quirk — it is a relational weapon.*

And women are the ones who bleed.

Chapter 2

WHY A TAXONOMY MATTERS

The Damaging Effects of Male Secrecy

Secrets are not harmless clutter — they are structural.

Here's the real sting — the part women know in their bones but rarely say aloud: *we've been trained to accept male secrecy as normal.*

We were taught to be patient, to be understanding, to "give him space," to not "nag," to not push too hard, to not be "dramatic."

We were told to carry the emotional truth of the relationship while he carried whatever truths he preferred to keep hidden.

But that burden? That quiet, invisible labor? That sickening feeling you get when you know something is wrong but he swears everything is fine?

That is not love. That is not partnership. That is *survival work.*

A man's secrecy forces women into roles they never signed up for:
Detective.
Therapist.

Mind reader.
Crisis manager.
Apologist.
Peacekeeper.

Meanwhile, he continues to believe he's "simple."

Male secrecy is real, rampant, and consequential.

Men's secrets are not incidental — they shape the world women have to live in.

Secrecy is not a flaw. It is a *system*.

A system that preserves *male comfort at the cost of women's clarity.*

The lies of omission, the locked emotional drawers, the conveniently forgotten histories... they alter the dynamic of every conversation, every conflict, every long night spent wondering why you feel lonely next to someone who insists he loves you.

What Women Lose While Men Stay Silent

1. The Emotional Price Tag
Every secret a man keeps requires a woman to *compensate* for it in some way—emotionally, mentally, or physically.

When he withholds feelings, she becomes the emotional detective.
When he hides money problems, she becomes the financial stabiliser.
When he lies by omission, she becomes the relationship's project manager.

His silence becomes her labor.

2. The Mental Load Explosion

A man's secret is never a single object. It's a branching system of consequences:

If he's hiding debt → she fears instability.

If he's hiding shame → she absorbs the emotional shrapnel.

If he's hiding resentment → she walks on eggshells without knowing why.

If he's hiding porn use → she questions her attractiveness, sexual prowess or sexual worth.

She feels the impact immediately.

He feels it only when the fallout lands on him.

3. The Erosion of Trust

Secrecy behaves like mould: You never see it at first—only the discoloration.

You sense a vibe shift, a "something's off," a hollow space in conversations.

But by the time you finally identify it, it has spread through the walls.

You can rebuild trust after honesty. You cannot rebuild trust after deception. One is repairable; the other is structural damage.

4. The Self-Blame Trap

Women in relationships with secret-keepers often fall into predictable, heartbreaking self-blame patterns:

"Maybe I'm overreacting."

"Maybe I'm too sensitive."

"Maybe I'm imagining things."

"Maybe he just needs space."

"Maybe it's my fault he's hiding things."

This is how secrecy mutates into self-doubt.

This is how smart, perceptive women learn to mistrust their own instincts.

The tragedy is not that men have secrets.

The tragedy is that *women are conditioned to think they're crazy for noticing.*

5. The Early Warning Signs You Should Never Ignore

Consider these the relationship equivalent of smoke under the door:

He becomes suddenly protective of his phone, or has a second, secret phone.

He makes sure his laptop screen is facing away from you.

He gets vague about how he spends time.

He answers questions with emotional evasiveness, not clarity.

He makes *you* feel guilty for asking normal questions.

He accuses you of "checking up on him" when you're just being a partner.

He compartmentalises parts of his life you're "not supposed to worry about".

Every one of these behaviours signals a boundary you did not agree to.

6. When Secrecy Signals Deep Structural Issues

Sometimes a secret is just a secret.

Often, it is a symptom:

Avoidant attachment

Addiction or shame cycles

Fear of intimacy

Lack of emotional skill

Entitlement

Immature conflict avoidance

Or simply a belief—conscious or unconscious—that you don't *deserve* the truth.

The why matters less than the impact: Secrets distort reality.

If you cannot trust what you are living inside, you cannot trust your life.

Here is the truth we will walk into together for the rest of this book:
You are not imagining it.
You are not paranoid.
You are not needy.
You are not demanding for wanting transparency.
You are not "too much".

You are asking for the bare minimum: A relationship where you are not left guessing. If that is too much for him, his secrets are only the beginning of the story.

Why a Taxonomy Matters
Because once you name a pattern, *you can no longer be gaslit by it.*

Once you recognise:
the shame-based secret
the convenient secret
the habitual secret
the ego-protecting secret
the male-culture secret
the big betrayal –

You begin to see your relationship clearly.

You begin to see *him* clearly.

But most importantly: You begin to see *yourself* clearly — not as someone who "puts up with too much," but as someone who has been navigating a maze she was never told existed.

This chapter is not about blaming women.

This chapter is your map.

The rest of the book will teach you how to navigate the terrain — without losing your mind or your sense of self in the process.

And if you've ever felt like you're fighting for clarity in a fog of half-truths...

Welcome. You've just stepped into the light.

Let's keep going.

Chapter 3

Secret Lives of Men

The Reflex of Secrecy

This is not a book about villains or predators or the stereotypical "bad man." In fact, the most surprising truth is this: Even the decent men—the reliable ones, the loving ones, the ones who mean no harm—have secret compartments.

Most aren't malicious. Many are left over from childhood. Some are shaped by shame, others by fear. A few are simply the product of the way boys grow into men in cultures that prize stoicism, silence, and emotional self-containment.

Men are trained from a young age to keep certain things to themselves: their weaknesses, their wants, their sexual histories, their failures, their worries about money, their private fantasies, their unresolved hurts.

By adulthood, secrecy becomes a reflex.

Women often interpret this as dishonesty.

Men often see it as self-protection.

Both perspectives make sense—but without translation, the gap between them becomes a breeding ground for confusion, mistrust, and needless pain.

Case Study: The Lie That Broke an Entire City's Hearts

This is a story, currently unfolding.

One that has left thousands of people incredulous, disgusted, and—if we're honest—no longer able to pretend that male secrecy is some cute personality quirk women should patiently tolerate.

It's a story that has shaken an Australian city and enraged the country—especially women.

It centres around a ten-year-old family dog. We'll call him Archie, not his real name. Loyal. Gentle. The kind of companion who sees you through babies, mortgages, work stress, everything.

In November 2025, Archie's owner – a seemingly credible, likeable, middle-aged married man – claimed that his vehicle had been stolen from the city's outskirts, while Archie was sleeping in the back.

The callous crime made national news. On television and social media, Archie's owners made tearful pleas to the perpetrators: You can keep the car, just PLEASE return our boy.

The public was heartbroken. Everyone rallied and offered donations. Volunteers searched. Strangers posted sightings. Police worked the case.

As the days passed with no sign of the stolen car or of Archie, dog-lovers held their breath.

Everyone was united in hope, and in disdain for the thieves. Who would do such a thing? It even sparked an online petition which gathered almost 50,000 signatures, calling for the introduction of a new law, making it a specific criminal offence to cause the death of an animal during another crime.

Nine days later, the utility vehicle was located, parked on an inner city street.

Archie was found inside. Deceased.

There was collective heartbreak. The city grieved for Archie's owners. People cried for a dog they'd never met, who didn't deserve to go like this. A beloved pet had suffered the worst imaginable fate—abducted, abandoned, alone, trapped, helpless.

Soon came the twist that turned grief into outrage: police alleged the vehicle was never stolen at all. CCTV footage indicated that the owner himself had parked it at the location late at night, left Archie inside, walked away, and then the next morning spun a story about a stolen vehicle to his wife, who had then notified police.

The public was confused. Social media posts were expressions of shock.

And then came another twist that turned sorrow and confusion into fury.

Media outlets claimed that Archie's owner had fabricated the story because, according to sex workers and other witnesses, he had patronised two brothels that night.

There had been no theft, but there had been a secret. A secret he did not want his wife to know.

He had gone to the extreme of spinning an elaborate story about his vehicle being stolen, misleading police, media and public for days, just to keep a secret locked away.

The full story will play out legally—but one fact has already landed like a punch to the chest: a deception, designed to hide personal behaviour, ended in tragedy. A lie created chaos. A secret ended a life and broke hearts.

A beloved dog died. A community was misled. And a woman – a wife – now sits with a truth that may be more devastating than the public will ever know.

Women saw it instantly for what it was: *the perfect embodiment of male secrecy.* How far some men will go to avoid the discomfort of honesty. How quickly they can endanger others rather than risk discovery or embarrassment. How even the lives that depend on them are collateral when protecting their hidden world.

Archie's story isn't an outlier. It's an extreme, horrible example of a pattern women know intimately: A man's secret rarely stays contained inside his head. Someone—often someone innocent—pays the price. In this case, it's the trusting wife and dog-Mom, grieving for the loss of her pet, as well as coming to terms with the ultimate and humiliating betrayal by a husband she thought she knew.

This is what male secrecy looks like when you strip away the polite euphemisms.

This is what happens when the "locked room" in a man's mind becomes more sacred than the living beings who love him.

This is the human cost—no, the *collateral damage*—of a man choosing secrecy over accountability.

Women often think men's secrets are small things: a hidden insecurity, an unspoken resentment, a private fantasy, a bit of shame they don't want exposed.

But secrets grow mold. Secrets require maintenance. Secrets warp everything around them.

And sometimes, secrets demand sacrifices—trust, safety, dignity, compassion, relationships, or in this case, the life of a dog or the love of a woman – who trusted the wrong man.

Archie is gone. His owner may face animal cruelty charges. But the story blew over.

This silence, this careful withholding of information, this gentle shielding of a man's path through the justice system is familiar. It's routine. It's the same old choreography we've seen all our lives.

The wrath of dog lovers, outraged animal-rights activists and public anger may be simmering under the surface, but men—especially men who lie—are protected as a matter of cultural reflex. We protect them because that is what society has always done. Even the ones with secret lives. Even the ones who want the best of both worlds: the furtive, paid-for sex as well as a respectable, devoted, pretty partner at home.

Women are the ones doubted, scrutinized, blamed. "Why did he feel the need to use sex workers?"

Women are the ones told they're overreacting. "It was just once." "It was harmless". "I was just drunk/drugged". "It didn't mean anything."

But a man? Even when the allegations are horrifying, when a community is grieving, when the story has spiralled into public heartbreak?

Society goes quiet, tucking the whole thing neatly behind closed institutional doors.

Not because of danger, nor outrage. But because a man is involved—and the machinery of our society still instinctively arranges itself to cushion him from the full weight of consequence.

That's what secrecy really looks like.

Not just the private lies men tell behind closed doors, but the collective, guilt-ridden, male complicity that rises up around them when those lies finally crack open.

This silence isn't about safety. It's about protection. The quiet, familiar protection society extends to men who lie.

Because that is what we do.

We protect them.

We hide for them.

We whisper "good man" long after their actions tell us otherwise.

And women know this dance by heart.

What Archie represents should never be forgotten: a devastating reminder that the hidden rooms of men's minds are not harmless spaces. They are chambers where self-preservation eclipses empathy, where truth is negotiable, and where other people—women, children, pets—can pay the price for what a man refuses to admit aloud.

And so, with Archie's story still heavy in the air, let's think about men and their secrets, Because every woman needs to understand what lies behind that locked shed at the back of a man's life.

***Author's Note:** This chapter discusses a publicly reported legal case involving an Australian resident. The individual is not named. All references are based on contemporaneous media reporting. No findings of guilt are asserted or implied. The purpose of this chapter is cultural and psychological analysis, not legal judgment.*

Chapter 4

The Hidden Rooms of a Man's Mind

And Why Women Don't Have the Keys

Every woman eventually learns, usually after much confusion, heartbreak, or quiet fury:

Men always have a room you're not allowed to enter. Always.

It's the emotional equivalent of a locked shed at the back of their lives—rusted padlock, missing key, and a suspicious insistence that *"there's nothing in there."*

That shed is where men store everything they don't want examined: past mistakes, embarrassments, shame, half-truths, hidden desires, emotional avoidance, and sometimes even habits they're too cowardly to admit.

And here's the kicker: the nicer he seems, the tighter the lock.

Society practically begs women to look the other way.

Men being "private" is treated as noble.

Men being evasive is excused as personality.

Men hiding things is reframed as "not wanting to worry you."

Women are encouraged to ignore this. We're told to trust, to be patient, to accept that men are "simple creatures" who "don't like to open up." Meanwhile, men are praised for silence, rewarded for evasion, and treated as delicate geniuses whose feelings must be tiptoed around so they don't retreat.

We're expected to cushion the secrecy, soften the silence, and "respect his boundaries"—even when those boundaries demand blindness.

We are trained to play along, to nod politely, to accept the locked room as normal instead of seeing it for what it is: a fortress built from fear, entitlement, and emotional laziness.

This book stops playing nice.

Women have been too generous for too long.

The Architecture of the Male Vault

Most men are raised to believe emotions are either weaknesses or weapons. Vulnerability is drilled out of them, emotion shamed, confession punished. So instead of developing a healthy internal world, they become emotional hoarders—stacking unprocessed feelings, shoving mistakes into corners, building an entire pantry labelled *DO NOT OPEN.*

And they expect women not to notice.

It would almost be sympathetic if it didn't spill so much debris into women's lives.

A boy who grows into a man who never learned introspection is like someone living in a house where all the doors are nailed shut. But empathy doesn't erase consequences.

His inability to metabolise truth becomes *your* problem. His fear of being seen becomes *your* confusion. His shame becomes *your* emotional labour.

Men don't compartmentalise because they're disciplined. They compartmentalise because they were never taught to confront themselves.

They've been trained to outsource the hard work of introspection—to mothers, girlfriends, wives, anyone but themselves.

And when women try to get close? They tighten the lock. Letting us see the mess would mean admitting it exists.

Why Women Put Up With It

Let's call this out directly: Women tolerate male secrecy because we've been trained to accommodate male comfort above our own clarity.

From girlhood, we are taught to:
- **Understand him.**

- **Be patient with him.**

- **Soften for him.**

- **Lower expectations.**

- **Smooth over disappointments.**

- **Interpret his moods.**

- **Walk on eggshells when he withdraws.**

- **Assume he is simple, fragile, and easily overwhelmed.**

- **Prioritise his peace over our truth.**

- **Not "nag", pressure him to talk or ask too many questions.**

There is no reciprocal training for men. They are not taught to decode women—they are taught to dismiss them. There is no cultural push to decode *our* silences.

So while women meticulously monitor a man's tone, silences, half-texts, inconsistencies, and mood shifts, men assume women are complicated and carry on.

It's astonishing that any heterosexual relationships survive at all.

Seeing Clearly Is Liberation

Here's your freedom: *You are not the locksmith for a man's emotional prison.*

If he wants to remain closed, let him. Your job is not to coax confessions or fix what another woman, his mother, or society failed to teach him.

Your job is simply to see clearly.

And seeing clearly begins with understanding that a man's hidden rooms are not anomalies—they are standard architecture. The question is not whether he has secrets.

The question is which ones, why, and what they cost you.

Once you see the system, you cannot un-see it. Once you name the pattern, you cannot fall for it again. Once you understand, you stop blaming yourself. Once you recognize what men hide and why, you step out of confusion and into clarity and power.

The case of Archie the dog, from the previous chapter, is extreme, yes. But the architecture of the lie — the concealment, the performance, the quiet confidence that everyone will believe his owner's lies until the truth is exposed — is *textbook* male secrecy.

This is what "good men" rely on:

- **Trust without verification.**

- **Belief without scrutiny.**

- **Sympathy without evidence.**

And women? We are trained to provide all three.

Even the so-called "good men" are hiding things—and women keep excusing them.

In the next chapters, we will explore why society teaches women to tolerate male secrecy, and why the price for doing so is far higher than we've been led to believe.

Chapter 5

Good Men, Quiet Secrets

Why Even the "Best" Men Are Still Hiding Something—and Why Women Keep Letting Them

Let's sharpen the blade for a moment. The myth of the "good man" isn't just a misunderstanding. It's a cultural survival mechanism — for men. It keeps them protected, insulated, unexamined, and endlessly forgiven. It gives them cover. It gives them loopholes. And, most importantly, it gives them women who doubt their own instincts before daring to doubt *him*.

Women cling to this myth the way society clings to fairy tales: stubbornly, desperately, and against all evidence. The "good man" is the last great cultural illusion — the emotional unicorn, the domesticated minotaur, the rare male specimen we're supposed to feel grateful for.

We cling to the idea of the "good man" because society gives us so few alternatives. We're taught that the world is full of monsters — so when we meet a man who doesn't scream, doesn't cheat, doesn't drink daily, and hasn't raised a hand, we're supposed to feel lucky. Blessed even. As though basic decency has become an endangered species.

A "good man" today usually means:

- **Doesn't cheat (that you know of).**

- **Doesn't yell (often).**

- **Doesn't drink himself into oblivion (regularly).**

- **Doesn't hit you (congratulations, apparently).**

- **Remembers to text back sometimes.**

- **Has the emotional range of a teaspoon but at least knows the word "therapy".**

The bar is so low it's subterranean. And still, women trip over it every day, because we're told it's the best we'll get – often by the men themselves.

Women call men "good" for behavior that should be *bare minimum human decency,* just as men use the word "babysitting" when having to look after their own kids.

The absurdity would be comical if it weren't the scaffolding of so many women's emotional lives.

Meanwhile, these same "good men" are carrying their quiet little secrets around like security blankets, trusting—correctly—that women will rationalize them away.

And women do. Not because we're naive but because we're conditioned to. We're trained to avoid conflict, to maintain harmony, to excuse what men refuse to name.

The Psychology of the "Good Man" — Why He Believes He Deserves Forgiveness

Here's the uncomfortable truth: the so-called good man rarely sees his secrecy as wrong. He sees it as *reasonable.* He sees it as *necessary.* And—this is the bitter pill—he sees it as *forgivable before he even does it.*

Why? Because women are raised to *earn* love—through effort, empathy, service, patience, and apology.

Men are raised to *feel entitled* to it.

From boyhood, the script begins:
He misbehaves → adults say "boys will be boys."
He hides something → adults laugh and call it mischief.
He's caught lying → adults praise him for being "clever" or "independent."
He avoids emotions → adults call him strong.
He withdraws → adults call him stoic.

By adulthood, secrecy feels less like a moral failing and more like a *normal, expected part of masculinity.*

Good men—especially good men—lean on this. They internalise a lifelong confidence that their lapses will be forgiven because the world has been forgiving them since they were toddlers.

They learn to expect grace. Women learn to provide it.

And this is the tragic, inevitable collision at the heart of heterosexual relationships: one gender is conditioned to confess, the other is conditioned to conceal.

The Hidden Curriculum of the "Good Man"

Here's the truth that stings: the "good man" image isn't just something women create. Men rely on it. They cultivate it. They hide behind it like a priest behind his pulpit.

Because as long as a man appears good — polite, presentable, occasionally thoughtful — his secrets are framed as harmless.

Women are encouraged to treat his omissions as quirks, his evasions as stress, and his inconsistencies as misunderstandings.

The "good man" label becomes a cloaking device. Once it's applied, it is almost impossible for women to remove.

This is why good men's secrets are the most dangerous of all. Big secrets are obvious; dramatic betrayals, glaring. But the "good man's" secrets blend. They slide into everyday life unnoticed, because the man wearing them has been pre-approved by society.

He is safe. He is decent. He is good.

And women are taught to never examine goodness too closely.

The Myth of the Good Man Is a Social Construct — Not a Reflection of Reality

The "good man" myth is not an observation. It's a *story*, meticulously crafted and culturally protected. Men don't have to earn the title — they simply have to avoid dramatic misbehavior.

The "good man" is a man who manages not to explode. He may be withholding, evasive, moody, inconsistent, passive-aggressive, or quietly resentful — but as long as he doesn't publicly implode, he is considered "good enough."

Women, meanwhile, are expected to be empathic Olympians — interpreting nuances, reading tones, smoothing over tension, and performing endless emotional acrobatics to keep the "good man" myth intact.

It's not that good men don't have secrets. It's that the *myth* says their secrets don't matter. That they're harmless. That women should rise above them.

And that is the real danger.

The Social Reward System That Lets Good Men Hide Better
Society rewards men for:

- **Silence.**

- **Withdrawal.**

- **Strategic vagueness.**

- **Emotional minimalism.**

- **Conflict avoidance.**

- **Being *slightly* less disappointing than the worst men.**

Good men are not good because they are transparent. They are good because they are *palatable.* Pleasant. Socially competent. Polite.

Their "goodness" is often a curated surface—a veneer.

Society rewards:

- **Charm.**

- **Mildness.**

- **Soft-spoken authority.**

- **The ability to appear calm under scrutiny.**

- **The talent for keeping uncomfortable truths private.**

In other words, good manners become camouflage.

And emotional silence? That becomes virtue.

A quiet man is seen as stable, wise, and self-controlled when in reality he may simply be unaccustomed—or unwilling—to tell the truth. Silence earns him credibility he hasn't actually earned.

Women mistake this quietness for emotional maturity, when it is frequently the opposite: a shield that prevents accountability.

So the good man hides more easily not because he is better, but because he is better *trained*. Better socially rewarded. Better protected by the narrative that says men who don't shout, cheat, or hit must be noble.

Goodness becomes a performance. Women become the audience expected to clap.

Why Women Confuse Goodness With Harmlessness
Here's the great trick of patriarchy: it teaches women that "good" and "harmless" are the same thing.

They aren't.

A man can be gentle, funny, polite, affectionate—and still hide things that will hurt you.

Good men may not cause chaos, but they cause confusion. Their secrets unfold slowly, subtly, quietly eroding women's confidence.

Women are taught to fear dramatic men and ignore the quietly evasive ones. But the softly-spoken secrets of a "good man" can be just as damaging, because:

- **You don't expect them.**

- **You don't prepare for them.**

- **You excuse them longer.**

- **You doubt yourself more.**

Good men get away with more because women *want* to believe in them.

Women are taught that if a man isn't cruel, he must be safe.

But harmlessness is not the same as honesty. And quiet men hide extremely well.

How Women Can Recognise the Difference Between Kindness and Concealment

Here is where women reclaim their perception.

A man's *kindness* makes your life easier. A man's *concealment* makes your life harder.

You can tell the difference by watching for:

1. Confusion

If you often feel confused, unsure, or vaguely on edge, something is being hidden. Confusion is the smoke of secrecy.

2. Inconsistency

A "good man" will give you a story that feels almost right—not quite right. A detail missing. A timeline fuzzy. A tone slightly too rehearsed.

3. Emotional Vacancy

Kind men engage. Concealing men retreat. Watch who he becomes when the truth is uncomfortable.

4. The Shift

When you ask a real question and his whole body changes—posture, eyes, tone—that is not kindness. That is defence.

5. Fragmented Honesty

If he gives you *pieces* of truth instead of the whole thing, he's not confused. He's curating.

These are not red flags of cruelty—they are *red flags of concealment*. Some of the most damaging secrets are kept by men who genuinely believe they are being good.

The Good Man's Secrets

The "good men" aren't usually the dramatic ones. They're the quietly evasive, polished ones.

The ones who don't technically lie — they simply curate, or conveniently leave bits out.

The ones who don't shout — they stonewall.

The ones who don't cheat — but keep an inner life you're not invited into.

The most dangerous secrets aren't the dramatic ones. Not all men are orchestrating double lives.

They're the little things men hide—the things women are told not to worry about, not to ask about, not to push about.

Their secrets are subtle, slippery, woven seamlessly into daily life.

They're poisonous because they're invisible and rationalized away:

- **Resentment left unspoken.**

- **Attraction un-admitted.**

- **Guilt undiscussed, buried under silence.**

- **Habits disguised as "nothing".**

- **Tiny betrayals dressed up as "white lies".**

- **The quiet refusal to confront past mistakes or exes.**

- **Insecurities they weaponize with silence.**

- **Fantasies they hope you'll never know.**

- **Relationships not harmless enough to not want you to stumble upon.**

- **Emotional needs he's outsourced.**

- **Private habits they don't want questioned.**

- **Choices he justifies as "protecting you" when they're really protecting his ego.**

These secrets are dangerous because women are trained to excuse them. To smooth over the edges. To rationalize the behaviour. To manage the fallout.

Women perform unpaid emotional labor that keeps men looking good while we navigate the consequences of their secrecy.

And because he's "nice," because he's "a good bloke," because he doesn't cheat, because he's better than the horror stories—women silence their instincts.

But here's the truth:
A man doesn't need to be malicious to be damaging.

A secret doesn't need to be criminal to corrode a relationship.

And most women's heartbreak isn't caused by betrayal—it's caused by being shut out.

None of this is scandalous enough for a TV drama. But it *is* corrosive enough to slowly erode the emotional health of the woman standing next to him.

Why Women Put Up With It
Let's call it what it is: women tolerate male secrecy because society trains us to accommodate men at all costs.

And we don't just tolerate it, we're rewarded for it.

Women are socially punished for confronting anything that disrupts male comfort.

From childhood, girls are taught to:

- **Make allowances for him.**

- **Interpret moods.**

- **Understand him.**

- **Be patient with him.**

- **Soothe him.**

- **Not "nag".**

- **Smooth over disappointments.**

- **Lower expectations.**

- **Prioritize his comfort over their clarity.**

Women meticulously monitor every detail: tone, pauses, half-texts, subtle shifts in mood.

Men, meanwhile, carry on. They are not trained for any of that. They're not raised to decode women. They're taught to dismiss, to evade, to expect women to absorb the fallout.

The system works beautifully — for them.

The Most Dangerous Secrets Are the Ones Women Excuse

These secrets are dangerous precisely because they don't look like secrets.

They look like:

"He's just stressed."

"He's tired from work."

"He didn't mean it that way."

"He's just private."

"He doesn't like conflict."

These are dangerous because they masquerade as nothing. Women smooth them over, rationalize them, and absorb the consequences. Women become translators, therapists, and emotional archaeologists — doing the excavation work men refuse to do.

Eventually, the excuses become part of our own personalities.

The Good Man's Favorite Weapon: Selective Honesty

Good men rarely lie outright. They avoid the risk.

Instead, they curate. They give you enough truth to keep you calm and withhold just enough detail to keep themselves comfortable.

They become experts in:

- **The half-confession.**

- **The vague story.**

- **The omission with a smile.**

- **The "forgot to mention".**

- **The "harmless" lie that protects their ego, not your heart.**

This may not be malicious. But it's strategic.

Men learn early: *full honesty risks consequences.*

Partial honesty keeps the peace. How many times have you heard the half-joking, "Happy wife, happy life"?

Women fall for this not because we're gullible, but because we're trained to feel *ungrateful* for wanting the whole truth.

We fear being labeled:

- **Dramatic.**

- **Paranoid.**

- **Overreacting.**

- **Needy.**

- **Insecure.**

- **Neurotic.**

So we stop asking questions.

And that is exactly how the myth of the "good man" survives.

Why His Quiet Secrets Hurt More Than His Loud Mistakes

A dramatic betrayal, paradoxically, brings clarity.

A quiet secret brings confusion.

Quiet secrets warp women's reality because they force us to interpret what he will not articulate. We see shifts in mood, lapses in honesty, subtle withdrawals, and we internalize them.

We ask ourselves:
Is he pulling away, or am I being dramatic?
Did he lie, or did I mishear?
Is something wrong, or am I imagining things?
Am I lacking in some way?

Men's quiet secrets outsource emotional detective work to women. A "good man" rarely feels guilty about this — because no one ever told him he should.

In fact, people *praise* him for being "easygoing" or "not like other men," even while he keeps women guessing, explaining, interpreting, and smoothing.

The Cost of Maintaining the Myth

When women cling to the idea of the good man, we pay in ways men never even notice.

Women shrink their intuition.
Women override their instincts.
Women silence their questions.
Women manage men's emotional loose ends like unpaid interns of the heart.

Every time a woman excuses a secret, she chips away a piece of herself: her clarity, her self-trust, her energy.

The myth of the good man doesn't just distort who he is.It distorts who *you* are allowed to be.

And the cost is high:

- **Emotional exhaustion.**

- **Self-doubt.**

- **Hypervigilance.**

- **Guilt for asking for basic transparency.**

- **The slow numbing of your own needs.**

When women stop tolerating the myth, men call it nagging. But it is simply this: *women choosing themselves.*

The Real Reason Women Keep Forgiving

It's not weakness. It's not naivety. It's social conditioning so deep it might as well be coded in bone.

Girls are trained from infancy to be relationship caretakers. Boys are trained to be relationship beneficiaries.

Women are taught that sacrificing clarity is noble. Men are taught that withholding clarity is normal.

Women are taught that asking for honesty is "pushing too hard." Men are taught that providing honesty is optional.

Women are taught to hold the emotional glue. Men are taught to expect the bond without ever touching the bottle.

So the "good man" isn't actually good — he's simply reassured that, whatever he hides, she will explain away.

The Most Dangerous Lie: "He Wouldn't Do That."

This single sentence has kept more women trapped, confused, heartbroken, and betrayed than any other phrase in modern language.

"He wouldn't do that" is the lullaby of internalized self-doubt.

Women say it because they want to believe it.

Because believing the alternative means re-evaluating the entire relationship.

Because the world will judge her acceptance faster than his deception.

Because the myth of the "good man" is easier to hold than the truth of the flawed one.

But men *do* do that. Every day. Quietly, politely, subtly — under the halo of goodness women lovingly maintain for them.

The Halo of the "Good Man" Is Built Entirely on Women's Emotional Labor

Let's be clear: Good men do not stay good on their own. They stay "good" because women perform unpaid emotional housekeeping behind the scenes.

Women do the reconciling, the explaining, the smoothing over. They anticipate, interpret, soften, explain, adapt, empathize, and repair. They fill in the gaps, stitch up the inconsistencies, iron out the contradictions.

A "good man" is often only good because a woman absorbs the fallout of his secrecy.

He doesn't lose his temper because she preemptively avoids conflict.

He doesn't withdraw because she gently coaxes him open.

He doesn't lie outright because she doesn't question the omissions.

He never has to change because she keeps changing for both of them.

Take that labor away — and see what remains.

When Women Stop Tolerating, Men Call It "Nagging"

Try a simple 2-part experiment:

1. Ask a direct question.

See how fast you're treated as:

- Irrational.

- Demanding.

- Paranoid.

- Unreasonable.

Men know exactly how to destabilize women's confidence.

2. Now try questioning a hidden detail, asking for clarity, pointing out a pattern.

What happens?

Men retreat into their favorite defences and gaslighting strategies: "You're overreacting" or worse, "You're crazy, it's all in your head."

- **Your valid question → becomes an overreaction.**

- **Something they don't want to discuss → becomes something they**

dismiss or get angry about (so it will be dismissed).

- **Your request for openness → becomes "you're too much".**

- **Naming a pattern → becomes "you're imagining things".**

This is not incompetence. This is social conditioning.

The cycle is elegant:
Male secrecy → Female self-doubt → Male comfort preserved.

The Most Feminist Thing You Can Do
Stop calling men "good" just for meeting the bare minimum, for simply **not being awful**.

A man who hides less is not inherently good.
A man who hides better is not inherently trustworthy.
A man who avoids conflict not peaceful; he is evasive.
A man who stays quiet is not calm; he is withholding.
A man who never admits fault is not strong; he is fragile.
A man who tells the truth only when cornered is not honest, he is strategic (Hello Arnie's owner).

Women deserve more than men who meet **the bare minimum**. They deserve clarity without excavation, honesty without interrogation, and respect without excuses

At some point, every woman has to decide whether she wants to keep tending the myth of the "good man" or start tending to herself.

Because the truth is this: a man doesn't become good because you excuse his silences, soften his sharp edges, or make peace with his half-truths.

He becomes good when he chooses accountability over comfort, clarity over concealment, truth over ego.

And if he won't? Then the most powerful thing a woman can do is stop carrying the burden of his hidden world and walk back into her own—lighter, clearer, and no longer mistaking minimal harm for genuine goodness.

The moment you stop protecting his secrecy, you start protecting your life.

The Question That Will Change Your Life
Ask the most important question you'll ever ask yourself:

If you stopped excusing the things he hides, would you still think he's a good man?

Sit with that.

The answer — whatever it is — will tell you more than anything he's ever volunteered.

Chapter 6

Masculine Shame: The Engine of Avoidance

Why Men Hide and Women Pay the Price

Let's be clear: men are not secretive because they're mysterious. They are not enigmatic. They are not deep. They are not complex puzzles waiting to be solved by the right patient woman.

They are secretive because they've been *trained to be ashamed of themselves.*

Shame is the engine behind the male "hidden room" – the silent, relentless force that drives secrecy, evasion, and avoidance. It is not about morality, intelligence, or character. It has nothing to do with integrity or maturity.

At its core, male secrecy is about fear. Fear of looking weak, foolish, emotional, vulnerable, needy, or too human for their own fragile egos.

Some men hide because they are self-protective. Some because they fear judgment. Some because they want to retain control.

But very few are hiding because they think it's wrong.

Shame in men is taught, not intrinsic. And secrecy is strategic, not incidental.

This is why good intentions don't matter. Even men who mean well can carry patterns of secrecy, half-truths, and avoidance that cost women emotional labor, clarity, and trust.

The Shame Curriculum

From the moment boys can walk and talk, society begins a relentless curriculum in shame.

It is structured, consistent, and brutal:
Crying? Not masculine.

Fear? Not manly.

Neediness? Pathetic.

Mistakes? Must be hidden.

Desire for closeness? Must be disguised.

Confusion? Must be ignored.

Every male is taught that showing, admitting, or exploring emotional truth is a failure.

So they construct their locked rooms where they shove every feeling that threatens to expose their humanity.

And then—because patriarchy is cruel—they're praised for it; called "strong", "stoic", "low maintenance."

Meanwhile, women are told we're "too emotional" when we dare to show the feelings men are punished for having.

And who pays for this curriculum?

Women do. Every day, in every relationship.

We watch men contort themselves around their own shame, and somehow *we* end up doing the emotional cleanup, the smoothing over, the rationalizing, the forgiving, the "It's fine, I understand"—even when it absolutely is not fine.

Women are expected to tolerate secrecy as part of the bargain for male comfort—and to never question the system that rewards it.

Avoidance Masquerading as Simplicity

Men may manifest simplicity. But they're not simple—they're strategic and avoidant.

Men have learned to appear steady, straightforward, and reasonable while their internal landscape is a swirling mess of unprocessed emotion, guilt, shame, and suppressed longing.

Women are accused of "overthinking" when we notice patterns that are *objectively obvious*:

He forgets to call → He's stressed, ashamed, or avoiding conflict.

He omits a detail → He's protecting his ego, not being helpful.

He withdraws emotionally → He's terrified of vulnerability.

Women label ourselves "sensitive" while men brand their avoidance as "just how they are."

The Patriarchy's Perfect Loop

Masculine shame is socially constructed, reinforced, and meticulously maintained. It is systemic, not accidental.

The loop is:

Boys are shamed for emotion → they learn secrecy.

Men hide mistakes, guilt, desire → women absorb consequences.

Women excuse behaviour → men remain unexamined.

Men are rewarded for avoidance → system repeats.

This is not an individual failing; it is cultural. And women are expected to uphold it with a smile.

Shame Is Strategic, Not Honest

Men rarely hide things because they're truly remorseful. Most hide because it maintains control.

Some are self-protective.

Some fear judgment.

Some want to avoid accountability.

Many hide because they know women will forgive, rationalize, or manage the fallout.

Shame in men is *taught*, not innate.

Secrecy is *strategic*, not accidental.

This is why "but he means well" is not enough.

Even men with good intentions can carry deeply ingrained patterns of avoidance that corrode trust and drain their partners dry.

Women: Stop Cleaning Up After Their Shame
Here is the feminist truth:
Women are not responsible for curing men of shame.

You are not required to:

- **Decode their evasions.**

- **Manage their silences.**

- **Compensate for their ego-protecting lies.**

- **Normalize what society has told them to hide.**

- **Absorb the emotional fallout of their avoidance.**

It's not your job to be his therapist, his mother, his emotional interpreter, or the crisis manager for his undeveloped inner world.

Recognising the system is liberating. You can stop carrying shame that was never yours to begin with. Seeing it clearly allows women to set boundaries and demand honesty without guilt.

Shame may drive avoidance, but **you do not have to absorb it**. You do not have to carry the weight of a man's inability to confront his own humanity.

Next Steps: Seeing Without Excusing

Understanding masculine shame is only the first step. The next step is choosing what you will and won't tolerate.

Pay attention:

Notice the patterns.

Name the evasions.

Stop rationalizing behaviours that shrink your intuition.

Stop cleaning up after his secrecy just to maintain peace.

When women stop participating in the system, the system cracks.

Secrecy loses its power.

Avoidance loses its charm.

Truth becomes the baseline—not the battle.

And relationships—or life without them—become radically clearer.

In the end, breaking the mythology of the "good man" is not an act of cynicism but an act of returning to yourself.

When you stop grading men on effort, excuses, or potential, you reclaim the quiet voice that always knew the difference between warmth and performance.

You stop rewarding charm as though it were character. You stop mistaking self-control for emotional depth. And slowly, you rebuild your instincts—no longer filtering them through what society insists you owe men, but through what you owe your own peace.

This is not the work of becoming hardened; it is the work of becoming *less willing to disappear.*

PART II – SECRETS MEN KEEP

Chapter 7

Secret Lives of Decent Men

Male Secrecy as a Cultural Inheritance

By now, the groundwork has been laid. You've learned how silence protects men, how society rewards their restraint but punishes women's expression, and how secrecy becomes a kind of inheritance—passed from man to man, father to son, friend to friend. So when we arrive at the so-called *decent men*, the ones who appear safe, stable, emotionally literate, you might hope—finally—for transparency, or at least reciprocity.

This chapter is not about cruelty or malice. It's about male secrecy as a cultural inheritance, an instinct acquired long before adulthood, long before any relationship begins. Decent men aren't exempt from it; they're often better at it.

But here is the truth the earlier chapters have been quietly preparing you for:

Even the decent men have secret lives.

Not dramatic double-lives, not cinematic betrayals—no. Their secrecy is subtler. Tastier. More socially acceptable. They conceal their impulses in politeness, their resentments in competence, their omissions in charm. The difference between the "toxic" man and the "decent" one is rarely that one lies and the other does not. It's that one lies loudly and the other lies beautifully.

This is the kind of concealment women are trained not to see—because noticing it feels ungrateful. Ungenerous. Disloyal. It also feels dangerously close to blasphemy: questioning the goodness of the men we are told to trust.

Yet seeing the truth is feminist work. And this chapter is your permission slip.

The Psychology of the "Good Man": Why He Believes He Deserves Forgiveness

From boyhood, men are told a story: *you are inherently worth loving, and when you falter, you should be forgiven.*

Women, by contrast, are told: *you must earn love, maintain it, repair it, and never strain it too much.*

This produces a quiet but powerful split:
Men expect forgiveness.

Women expect to work for it.

A decent man might never say this aloud—many aren't even conscious of it—but the entitlement lingers under the surface. He apologises for the small offences, the easy ones, because they make him look accountable. But the deeper things—the private cravings, the old shame, the resentments he nurses quietly—those he tucks behind his ribs, out of reach. He believes you should trust him anyway. That he *deserves* that trust because he is "good."

And women, having spent their lives earning love, often accept this imbalance without question.

The Social Reward System: How Good Men Hide Better

Decent men don't appear secretive. Why? Because they've been culturally rewarded for the skills that conceal secrets:

Good manners as camouflage.

A polite man disarms suspicion.

His gentleness becomes the alibi for his omissions.

Emotional silence as virtue.

A quiet man seems stable, centred, thoughtful.

Rarely do people ask: What is he *not* saying?

Competence as character.

A man who pays bills on time and cooks pasta on Saturday nights is assumed trustworthy—even though reliability is not the same as transparency.

Society does not suspect the man who appears decent.

Women, trained to interpret politeness as moral character, suspect him even less.

And so the decent men carry their secrets in peace.

Why Women Confuse Goodness with Harmlessness

Women are raised, in explicit and subtle ways, to admire goodness in men as though it guarantees safety. But goodness and harmlessness are not synonyms. Many "good men" are harmless only because they've never encountered a situation where their secrecy costs them anything.

Their unspoken beliefs remain untested.

Their habits of concealment remain unexposed.

Their resentments remain unprovoked.

A good man is not harmless; he is unchallenged.

This explains why so many women feel blindsided later—after years of quiet inconsistencies, moments of defensiveness, or sudden revelations that force a re-evaluation of the entire relationship. He didn't become secretive overnight.

You simply stopped mistaking goodness for transparency.

Recognizing Kindness vs. Concealment

Clarity is not paranoia.

You're not looking for crimes—you're looking for patterns.

Women are often discouraged from trusting their intuition, especially when it conflicts with a man's polished surface. But intuition is pattern recognition in disguise. It notices what politeness tries to hide.

Signals of concealment often look like:

A kind man who cannot answer a simple question without a long exhale.

A polite man who becomes oddly protective of his digital life.

A generous man who never talks about his past but claims there is "nothing to say."

A charming man whose stories regularly shift by a degree or two.

A reliable man who bristles when you ask for clarity.

These behaviours don't reveal malice—they reveal *avoidance*. And avoidance is the backbone of secrecy.

Women break the pattern the moment they stop excusing avoidance as shyness, kindness, or "just how men are."

Patterns and Red Flags That Indicate Hidden Rooms

These are not accusations—merely indicators:

Vague answers to direct questions.

Defensiveness over small inquiries.

Selective disclosure of his social world.

Chronic minimisation or "forgetfulness."

Inconsistent stories.

Excessive charisma in moments where honesty is required.

Women are trained to overlook these signs. This chapter asks you not to.

While each man has his own biography, certain forms of secrecy are shockingly consistent:

1. The Past He Won't Talk About

The good man will speak about his past like a diplomat—strategically, selectively, and with a remarkable gift for vagueness.

Carefully edited histories. Missing context. Names swapped for pronouns.

Not lying—just softening, redirecting, omitting.

Red flags:

"I just don't like talking about the past."

Blurred timelines, strategic forgetfulness.

Stories that change slightly with each retelling.

Defensiveness over neutral questions.

2. The Hidden Desires

The decent man often hides desires he fears will disrupt the image he maintains.

Not necessarily dark impulses—more often mundane, human confusions or attractions he's ashamed of, sometimes immature, occasionally unprocessed.

Red flags:

"I was only joking" comments.

Jokes that sound like disclosures in disguise.

Anxious secrecy with digital life.

Over-explaining why something "doesn't mean anything".

3. The Emotional Evasion

Resentments are filed away like unpaid bills, surfacing only in tone or withdrawal.

He avoids conflict like a sport. He hates "big conversations."

He prefers silence over honesty—not because he doesn't care, but because he hasn't learned how to be uncomfortable without feeling attacked.

Red flags:

"It's fine" or "Nothing's wrong" when everything is.

"I don't want to get into it."

A quiet resentment you can sense but never locate.

4. The Curated Persona

This is the hallmark of the decent man.

He is the version of himself he wishes to be, rather than the one he is. The more perfect the presentation, the more scaffolding behind it.

Red flags:

Contradictions, rehearsed narratives, tiny slips – inconsistencies that are subtle but persistent.

Surprises that feel *off-brand.*

The sense that he's *performing* goodness, not living it.

5. The Ego-Protective Lies

These lies are rarely malicious. They're self-defensive—concealing embarrassment, insecurity, or fear of being perceived as inadequate.

Lies that protect not you, but his self-image.

Red flags:

Emotional volatility when questioned: defensiveness, escalation, or disproportionate irritation.

Minimising.

Changing small details.

None of these patterns make him a bad man. But they do make him a man with secrets.

Why This Matters: Recognising Patterns Is Feminist Work

Patriarchal cultures protect men from the discomfort of disclosure. They do not protect the women who live with the consequences.

This isn't about demonising men. It's about *lifting the burden of emotional blindness off women.*

Recognising secrecy in decent men is not bitterness. It's not cynicism. It is *survival.*

Recognising patterns is a form of self-preservation because it:
Reclaims your power.

Reclaims your clarity.

Reclaims your time.

Rebuilds your intuition.

Ends the unpaid emotional labour of deciphering another adult's inner life.

It says:
You are not overreacting.

You are not imagining gaps.

You are not meant to live inside someone else's unspoken world.

It is acceptable to expect transparency. Seeing clearly is the first step.

Boundaries are the second. It is acceptable to set boundaries.

It is acceptable to decline the role of emotional archaeologist. Not apologising for those boundaries is the third.

When you see the patterns:
Name what is happening.

Stop excusing omissions that drain you.

And insist—not quietly, not apologetically—on relationships built on clarity rather than illusion.

That is the work.

And that is your liberation.

Decent Men vs. Honest Men

The distinction matters. The difference is courage, not character.

A decent man avoids harm.
An honest man risks discomfort to prevent it.

A decent man behaves well.
An honest man lives transparently.

Decency is performative.

Honesty is lived.

Women have spent decades confusing the former for the latter.

But honesty is not a luxury.

It is the material from which real intimacy is built.

Reflective Exercise: The Clarity Checklist

Use this to assess whether you are in a relationship with a curated man or a transparent one:

1. When you ask a direct question, does he answer clearly or redirect?

2. Are you often left to "fill in the blanks" on your own?

3. Do you feel more like an interpreter than a partner?

4. Is his politeness a shield rather than an expression of openness?

5. Do you sense resentment beneath the calm surface?

6. Does he apologise only after being confronted, never proactively?

7. Do you find yourself shrinking your needs to maintain harmony?

8. When something feels off, does he reassure you verbally—or does he simply deny your intuition?

If more than half of these resonate, you're likely dealing with a man who is decent—but not honest.

And that distinction will shape the emotional cost of the relationship more than any other.

Takeaway

Even the most decent men have secret lives—not because they are villains, but because they were raised in a culture that teaches them to hide: their shame, their impulses, their fears, their failings. Women, meanwhile, are raised to fill in these missing pieces, to do the emotional excavation he avoids.

You cannot force a man into honesty.

But you *can* refuse to carry the cost of his secrecy.

In the end, seeing the secret lives of "decent men" is not about becoming suspicious—it's about becoming fluent. Fluent in patterns, fluent in your own intuition, fluent in the difference between kindness and concealment.

The more clearly you see, the less likely you are to lose yourself inside someone else's curated version of the truth.

And from that clarity comes the quiet, radical freedom to walk toward relationships that feel expansive rather than managed—where honesty is not a performance but a practice.

Chapter 8

The Cost of Secrets

Emotional Labor, Trust, and the Invisible Work Women Do

Every secret a man keeps creates an emotional invoice—for someone else.

Women absorb the fallout quietly, automatically. We're trained to view male secrecy as normal, even inevitable.

Let's talk about the price women pay for male secrecy. Spoiler: it is staggering, unacknowledged, and entirely normalized.

The Cost to Women

Women pay in:

Emotional labor: deciphering moods, reading silences, soothing tension; decoding what he won't say.

Self-doubt: thinking *you* are the over-thinker; wondering if this is "normal" or if you're imagining things.

Time and energy: managing what he won't; maintaining a relationship that requires translation.

Diminished intuition: ignoring what you feel because he insists nothing is wrong; the slow erosion of trust in your own perceptions.

And the bitter irony? The more decent he seems, the more invisible your work becomes.

Because he's not "doing anything wrong," right? He's just not saying it.

Case Study: Unspoken vulnerabilities

Sophie, 38, saw her husband Matt, 43, wincing when he rotated his shoulder. He denied it. She noticed his shortness of breath when out walking. Denied again. He insisted he was "fine, fine, FINE", snapping at her in an attempt to shut down the conversation.

A week later, she found him sitting on the edge of the bed in the early morning, gripping his chest. Still — he insisted it was "heartburn."

It wasn't.

It was a cardiac issue that could have killed him.

The cardiologist later told Sophie, "This should have been brought in much earlier."

Sophie wanted to scream. Brought in by whom? She wasn't allowed to know anything. She was the last to be told, yet expected to be the first to cope.

Her summary was blistering: "Men think secrecy protects us. What it actually does is turn women into unpaid first responders."

She added, "Being widowed before 40 would not actually qualify as *being protected!*"

The impact?

Fear, weaponised by silence.

A sense of constantly managing a secret she didn't choose.

Emotional labour multiplied by ignorance.

Every secret a man keeps, no matter how "small" or "harmless," even under the guise of protection a partner or hiding vulnerability, lands on the woman in his orbit. And because society insists women must manage men's egos, protect their feelings, and interpret their silences, this cost is invisible, unpaid, and emotional.

Emotional Labor: The Invisible Tax

Women perform emotional labor constantly, often without realizing it. Examples include:

Decoding moods: interpreting sighs, pauses, and tone.

Rationalizing evasions: "He didn't mean it that way."

Smoothing over inconsistencies: covering for forgotten promises or omissions.

Managing his comfort: staying calm when he avoids conflict, changes the subject, or hides something.

Absorbing guilt: feeling responsible for his secrets, even when they're not yours.

This labor is exhausting. It consumes energy, clarity, and patience. And the kicker? It is always invisible to the man doing the hiding.

Trust Is the Collateral Damage

Secrets erode trust. Even if a man is "good," each omission chips away at the foundation of the relationship. The pattern is subtle, cumulative:

He says one thing, but you sense another.

Stories don't add up, but you excuse it.

Facts appear later, leaving you wondering what else you don't know.

Women are trained to tolerate these inconsistencies. We are socialized to smooth over, rationalize, and pretend the system is fair. It isn't. Every hidden detail diminishes trust, and women carry the burden of staying sane while the man stays comfortable.

The Invisible Work That Becomes the Norm

Consider this: a "decent" man keeps secrets. A woman discovers them. She forgives or excuses. She adapts. She absorbs. She explains away. She accommodates.

What happens next?

The man feels no consequence.

The woman internalizes the emotional cost.

The pattern repeats.

This is the system working exactly as intended. Women maintain it by managing the fallout, often without ever recognizing that they are doing the labor of secrecy management for someone else.

Case Study: Micro-secrecies, emotional triangulation

Jess, 26, wasn't worried at first when her partner Sam, 25, started keeping his phone on silent. Everyone does that sometimes. But then came the additional little moves: phone turned face-down, notifications disabled, a new password.

When she asked about it, Sam rolled his eyes:

"Why are you so paranoid?"

But Jess wasn't paranoid; she was observant. She wasn't imagining the sudden late-night texting, the unexplained "work chats," or the moments he'd angle the screen away from her like a teenager hiding TikToks in a classroom.

What she later discovered wasn't an affair — but it was still a betrayal. Sam had been sharing his thoughts and private frustrations with a married female colleague who referred to herself as his "work wife".

Jess said: "He was building an emotional world I wasn't allowed in. I was being edited out of my own relationship."

The impact?

Erosion of trust
Feeling gaslit ("you're overreacting")
A sense of humiliation
Being cast as a villain in someone else's story.

Why Women Should Stop Excusing It

Here is the feminist reality: women are not obligated to absorb the consequences of someone else's shame, ego, or avoidance. Secrets cost energy, clarity, and trust. Women are entitled to:

Expect honesty without excavation.

Demand transparency without guilt.

Refuse to rationalize omissions or half-truths.

Stop performing unpaid labor that enables secrecy.

When women stop excusing hidden rooms, the power shifts. Secrecy loses its comfort. Evasion loses its reward. And the "good man" either grows up—or remains only as good as his ability to hide.

The Systemic Angle

Let's be clear: this isn't just about individual men. This is a cultural pattern reinforced across generations.

Boys are shamed for vulnerability → Men grow up hiding.

Men hide → Women absorb.

Women absorb → Men stay comfortable.

Society praises "decent" men for minimal harm → the loop continues.

The cost is cumulative: women carry the emotional fallout of male secrecy for decades, sometimes unconsciously. The toll? Anxiety, self-doubt, exhaustion, and diminished clarity about what they deserve.

The Feminist Solution

The solution is not perfection, patience, or turning men into confessing saints. The solution is clarity, boundaries, and accountability:

See the patterns clearly. Recognize hidden rooms, evasions, and omissions.

Name the consequences. Understand how secrecy affects your emotional life.

Stop excusing it. Refuse to absorb labor that is not yours.

Demand honesty, or disengage. Your energy, trust, and clarity are not negotiable.

Once women embrace this truth, the emotional economy shifts. Secrets no longer carry automatic power. Excuses no longer have a free pass. Women stop doing labor they were never meant to do.

Takeaway

Male secrecy comes at a price. Women pay it. Societal norms insist it is acceptable. But it isn't.

Your clarity, your time, your energy, and your trust are yours—not the collateral for a man's ego or shame. Recognizing the cost is the first step. Refusing to carry it is revolutionary.

PART III – FEMALE MISINTERPRETATION

Chapter 9

THE STORIES WOMEN TELL THEMSELVES

You're Not Overthinking. You're Noticing.

Overthinking vs Intuition

Women are not wrong about men's secrecy. But we are often wrong about what it means, where it comes from, and—most dangerously—what we are expected to do about it.

This chapter is not about absolving men. It is about understanding the psychological trap women are pushed into once male secrecy enters the room. Because long before a woman blames a man for his silence, she has usually been trained to blame herself.

Men hide.

Women interpret.

And somewhere in that gap, women lose clarity, confidence, and time.

Not All Secrets Are Personal (But That Doesn't Make Them Harmless)
One of the most destabilising things a woman learns in intimate relationships

is this: his secrecy may have nothing to do with you.

That sounds comforting. It isn't.

Women Interpret secrecy as betrayal. We are relationally socialised. We're taught that intimacy is built through disclosure, mutuality, and emotional transparency. So when a man withdraws, withholds, or deflects, women instinctively read this as a relational signal.

If he's hiding something, it must be:
- **About another woman.**

- **About his feelings for me.**

- **About something I did wrong.**

This interpretation isn't paranoia. It's pattern recognition shaped by how women are taught relationships work.

The problem is that male secrecy often isn't relational at all.

Men's Secrecy Is Often About Themselves, Not Their Partner

Many men hide not because they are actively deceiving their partners, but because they are:
- **Ashamed**

- **Avoidant**

- **Emotionally underdeveloped**

- **Protecting ego**

- **Resisting self-examination**

Their secrecy is internal, not strategic. It is about *not wanting to look at themselves,* not about managing the relationship.

But here's the crucial point: A secret that isn't "about you" can still profoundly affect you.

Men's internal avoidance spills outward. Silence creates instability. Withholding erodes trust. Emotional absence leaves women guessing. Whether or not the secret is personal, the *impact always is*.

The Emotional Translation Gap

Women speak emotion fluently. Men are often semi-literate.

So women attempt translation:
"He's quiet — maybe he's stressed."
"He snapped — maybe he's tired."
"He withdrew — maybe I asked too much."

Women translate male behavior into relational language, because that is the only language we were taught.

Men, meanwhile, often experience their inner lives as foggy, compartmentalised, or irrelevant to others. They do not feel an urgent need to articulate or resolve emotional states before continuing with life.

This creates a brutal mismatch:

- **Women seek meaning.**

- **Men seek avoidance.**

- **Women fill in the gaps.**

And that's where the trouble begins.

The Stories Women Tell Themselves (In Order to Stay)

When clarity is unavailable, the human mind creates narrative. Women are exceptionally good at this—because we have had to be.

Women are told they "overthink."

Men are told they are "simple."

We've already established that this is one of the great gaslighting myths of heterosexual life.

What women call "overthinking" is often *pattern recognition without confirmation*. It is the mind circling unanswered questions because something doesn't add up.

Intuition notices:

- **Inconsistency**

- **Emotional withdrawal**

- **Misalignment between words and behavior.**

But intuition needs evidence to settle. When men refuse to provide clarity, women are left suspended—aware something is wrong, but unable to name it. Society then punishes women for this discomfort by calling it *neurosis*.

Attachment Style Reactions

Modern psychology has given women a new way to blame themselves: attachment theory.

Suddenly, male secrecy is reframed as:

- **Your anxious attachment.**

- **Your fear of abandonment.**

- **Your need for reassurance.**

Attachment theory can be useful. It can also be weaponized.

Too often, women are encouraged to self-regulate in response to male withdrawal, rather than question why withdrawal is acceptable in the first place.

Men's avoidance becomes women's pathology.

When Women Absorb Blame for Male Silence

This is the most damaging story women tell themselves: "If I were calmer, less emotional, more patient, more secure... he would open up."

So women:

- **Ask more gently.**

- **Demand less.**

- **Lower expectations.**

- **Stop asking altogether.**

Male silence is preserved. Female self-erasure is rewarded.

And the relationship appears "stable," at the cost of one person's inner life being steadily minimised.

The Feminist Reframe

Here is the uncomfortable truth this chapter asks you to hold: Men's secrecy may not be about you.

But *managing it* has been made your responsibility.

Understanding male psychology is not a call to tolerate harm. It is a call to stop misdirecting your energy.

You are not wrong for wanting clarity or noticing what isn't being said.

You are not broken for sensing distance.

The work is not to interpret men better.

The work is to *stop interpreting at all.*

Silence is information.

Avoidance is an answer.

Withholding is a choice.

Once women stop translating men's inner worlds for them, a profound shift occurs: Men are forced to confront themselves—or lose access to women who no longer do the emotional labour on their behalf.

And that, more than any conversation, is where truth finally begins.

Chapter 10

Focusing on Patterns

Red Flags vs Red Herrings

By now, it should be painfully obvious: men hide things. Even decent men. Even the ones who appear transparent, honest, and harmless.

And women, socialized to excuse, absorb, and rationalize, often fail to see it coming.

It's time to *stop pretending you're overreacting* and start reading the signals clearly. We've discussed red flags. This is how to interpret them .

Red Flags: What to Watch For

Not all secrets are sinister, but all of them cost you energy. Recognizing these patterns is self-preservation, not paranoia.

Red flags include:

Vagueness or Evasion: He dodges direct questions or changes the subject.

Defensiveness: A minor question about his past or behavior triggers disproportionate irritation.

Selective Transparency: He shares only what's convenient, never what's important.

Inconsistencies: Stories that don't quite line up, forgotten details, subtle contradictions.

Digital Obfuscation: Excessive secrecy around phones, emails, or social media.

Emotional Withdrawal: Refusal to discuss feelings, avoidant behavior, or prolonged silence.

Charm as a Shield: Excessive politeness or humor when you press for honesty.

Notice these patterns early. Don't rationalize, don't excuse, don't assume "it's fine." Seeing them clearly is your feminist map to navigating the hidden rooms of his life.

Patterns of Male Secrecy

Red flags alone don't tell the whole story. Look for *patterns,* because secrets are rarely isolated:

The Past He Refuses to Discuss

Exes, failures, embarrassing events—anything he expects you to forget or never ask.

The Half-Truth Specialist

Omits details, curates narratives, and tells you what *he thinks you can handle.*

The Emotional Ghost

Keeps silent about resentment, desire, or disappointment. Uses absence as a shield.

The Comfort-Seeker

Avoids accountability, asks you to absorb frustration, and rarely acknowledges impact.

The Evasion Maestro

Skillfully deflects, distracts, or reframes conversations to keep you from seeing the full truth.

Patterns matter. Single instances can be excuses, but repetition reveals *strategy, training, and priorities.*

Mapping Your Response

The feminist map is simple, even if society wants to convince you it's complicated:

See Clearly

Identify red flags and patterns. Don't minimize them.

Name the Consequences

Understand how his secrecy affects your emotional health, trust, and clarity.

Set Boundaries

Decide what behavior you will tolerate. Communicate it without apology.

Stop Excusing

Refuse to perform labor that is not yours. Do not rationalize evasions.

Decide Your Engagement

Honest confrontation, accountability, or exit—choose what preserves your energy.

Protect Your Energy

Emotional labor is finite. Stop expending it on someone who refuses to earn transparency.

A Feminist Truth

Here is the unvarnished, scornful truth: men have secrets. Women carry the fallout. But you do not have to. The red flags, the patterns, and the map exist so you can reclaim your clarity, your trust, and your power.

Recognizing this is revolutionary.

Seeing clearly doesn't make you cynical. It makes you self-respecting, informed, and unstoppable.

Remember: a man's comfort is not your responsibility.

His secrets are not your fault.

Your energy is not his playground.

Actionable Tools

Now that you know the red flags and patterns, we'll soon examine practical strategies for navigating relationships with men—how to ask questions, demand honesty, set boundaries, and disengage from secrecy without guilt.

PART IV – WHEN SECRETS BECOME DANGEROUS

Chapter 11

THE DARKEST CORNERS

Big Betrayal and Life-Changing Secrets

I n the **Taxonomy of Male Secrets,** there is a category that does not merely disappoint or confuse—it *restructures reality.*

These are not omissions.

They are not half-truths.

They are not the quiet evasions women are trained to tolerate.

These are the Big Betrayal Secrets
The ones that can change everything and make you question everything, from your judgement to your sanity.

The kind of thing that, once uncovered, rewrites the entire story of your relationship.

The kind of secret that detonates.

Some secrets change the emotional climate of a relationship. Others *level it.*

The most common of these detonations include:

- **Infidelity and long-term physical affairs.**

- **Secret children or parallel families.**

- **Financial infidelity, hidden debts, secret gambling.**

- **Concealed drug or alcohol addictions.**

Case Study: Financial secrecy (hidden accounts, concealed debts)
Jenna, 34, discovered her husband Will, 37, had a secret credit card when the bank called to confirm an overdue payment.

Will waved it off as "no big deal" — just a small balance, nothing to worry about.

Until a month later, a still-suspicious Jenna opened a letter addressed to Will and saw the real balance: $58,000.

The secrecy hit her harder than the debt: "We were supposed to be planning a future," she said, "and he'd been secretly gambling away our savings."

When Jenna confronted Will, he tried turning the tables with vicious accusations about her "snooping at his mail", followed classic male defensive minimalism:

"It's all under control"

"I didn't tell you because I didn't want you to stress."

But now Jenna *was* stressed — because she found herself living in a financial reality she hadn't even known she was part of.

The impact on her?

A sudden, cold sense that she'd been married to a stranger.

Hypervigilance around money.

Steps to regain control of her own financial independence.

Jenna eventually said, "It wasn't the money. It was being lied to by omission, drip by drip, until the slow leak of trust turned in to a dam burst we couldn't recover from."

The Darkest Corners of the Hidden Rooms

There's a more sinister category lurking here: the secrets society prefers not to look at directly.

- **Serious criminal behaviour.**

- **Sexual violence and exploitation.**

- **Crimes involving or exploiting children.**

- **Trafficking, coercion, or other forms of extreme harm.**

When a Big Betrayal secret is exposed, women often describe the same sensation: *vertigo*.

The past becomes unstable. The unsuspecting woman replays every memory with new eyes. Ordinary memories turn suspicious. Small details suddenly feel charged with meaning.

When these secrets surface, women do not simply learn something new.

They discover that the relationship they thought they were in never truly existed.

These secrets are not simply private failures. They are *structural lies*—entire lives built alongside the one a woman thought she was sharing.

The Moment Everything Rewrites
She questions herself.

Was any of it real?

Who was I actually living with?

What else don't I know?

This is not dramatics. This is a nervous system responding to the collapse of narrative safety.

Trust is not just emotional—it is cognitive. When it breaks, the mind scrambles to restore order.

The Secondary Wound: Shame
What follows the initial shock is often more insidious.

She does not blame herself — not consciously. But she often feels profound shame.

Shame for not seeing it sooner.

Shame for trusting.

Shame for believing the relationship was safe.

Shame for being associated with, maybe even being seen as protecting, the perpetrator.

This shame is not innate. It is imposed. The unspoken questions begin almost immediately:

How could she not have known?

What kind of woman misses something like that?

Was she naïve—or complicit?

The scrutiny rarely focuses on the man's decades of concealment, social camouflage, or institutional protection. It focuses on the woman who loved him.

She will feel the heavy burden of judgement (how could she not have known?) and humiliation (for not noticing).

Fear Joins the Room

Alongside shame comes fear. Not abstract fear—*practical, embodied fear.*

Fear for her own safety.

Fear for her children.

Fear for her reputation, livelihood, future.

The home that once felt familiar becomes charged. The relationship that once offered security becomes a source of threat.

Women are expected to process this quietly, rationally, with dignity—while their entire sense of reality is being rebuilt from the ground up.

The Myth That Makes This Possible
These secrets flourish in the shadow of a cultural lie: that harm is obvious, monstrous, and easy to spot.

In reality, many of the most dangerous secrets coexist comfortably with:

- **Kindness**

- **Respectability**

- **Gentleness**

- **Professional success**

- **Social trust**

Men do not need to be visibly cruel to cause devastating harm. They only need to be *believed.*

And women are trained to believe.

What Women Are Actually Responsible For (And What They Aren't)
Here is what must be said clearly:

You are not responsible for uncovering crimes you were actively shielded from.

You are not responsible for anticipating deception built on years of practice.

You are not responsible for intuiting what was deliberately hidden.

Trusting is not a moral failure.

Being deceived is not a character flaw.

The shame belongs where the secrecy lived.

When Secrets Become Dangerous

The danger is not just the secret itself.

The danger is the *system that normalises male secrecy and then punishes women for believing the performance.*

These are not cautionary tales about women needing to be smarter.

They are indictments of a culture that teaches men to hide—and teaches women to carry the consequences.

When the darkest corners are finally exposed, the most radical act a woman can perform is not self-blame, silence, or loyalty.

It is *clarity.*

Seeing what was hidden. Naming what was done.

And refusing to carry shame that was never hers to hold.

Because once a secret detonates, the truth does not ask to be managed.

It asks to be *faced*.

Chapter 12

A Shattered Archetype

The Man We Least Suspected

There are men we are taught to fear, and men we are taught to trust.

The frightening ones are obvious. They are loud in their failures. Their edges are rough. They fit easily into our mental categories of danger. When they disappoint us, the disappointment feels almost orderly.

Then there are the others.

The men whose work centres children. Innocence. Imagination. Care. The men whose public lives seem designed to reassure us that gentleness and masculinity can coexist without threat.

These men do not merely pass unnoticed; they are held up. Celebrated. Offered as proof.

When allegations surface against such a man, the shock is rarely about the alleged behaviour alone. It is about the collapse of a story we relied on.

This chapter is not about guilt or innocence. That belongs to the courts. It is about why women are so often encouraged to trust *archetypes* instead of patterns, and what happens when one of those archetypes shatters.

The Archetype That Disarms Us

The man at the centre of this case occupied a cultural role saturated with moral safety. His professional identity was intertwined with childhood, education, and emotional insight. His work lived in classrooms and family homes. Parents trusted him without ever needing to articulate why.

This is how archetypes function. They bypass analysis.

When a man fits a role we associate with goodness, scrutiny does not vanish. It simply feels inappropriate. Suspicion becomes impolite. Questions feel like accusations.

Women are especially trained to override their instincts in these moments. To tell themselves they are being unfair. Ungenerous. That their unease must say more about them than about him.

After all, look at what he does. Look at who he helps. Look at what he represents.

The archetype does the work.

Case Study: When the Safest Man in the Room Is No Longer Certain

In early 2026, Australian media reported that a widely admired author, married, with young children, and long associated with successful feel-good or coming-of-age stories and screenplays that were loved and embraced by educational institutions and families, had been charged with alleged child exploitation offences.

Reporting emphasised the presumption of innocence. The language was careful. The facts were limited to what had occurred procedurally.

According to court reports, police executed a search warrant at the man's home and seized electronic devices as part of an investigation involving alleged online activity. He appeared before a magistrate. The matter was adjourned. Further dates were scheduled.

Legally, nothing extraordinary occurred. The system moved slowly and deliberately, as it is designed to do.

Socially, the response was immediate and revealing.

Publishers paused promotional activity. Schools quietly reassessed reading lists. Educators and child-development specialists appeared in the media, not to speculate on guilt, but to help adults navigate conversations with children about uncertainty and trust.

Parents asked themselves questions they had never expected to ask: what to keep, what to remove, how to separate work from author, whether such a separation was even possible.

What fractured was not just confidence in one man, but faith in a category.

Public discussion quickly split. Some clung fiercely to the man's reputation, invoking his character, his contribution, his perceived nature as though these were counterweights on a scale.

Others, particularly women, felt something quieter but deeper: a recognition they had encountered before: that the men who surprise us most are often the ones we felt safest with. This is not a legal observation. It is a psychological one.

We want goodness to be visible. We want harm to look harmful.

And when a man's public persona has been built around care and innocence, the possibility of concealed behaviour feels not just distressing, but almost taboo to contemplate.

The courts will determine what is proven. But the cultural lesson does not require a verdict.

Reputation is not verification.

Respectability Is Not a Safeguard

One of the most persistent myths about male wrongdoing is that it comes from obvious places. From chaos. From men who are visibly damaged or socially marginal.

In reality, many forms of harm emerge from stability. From men who are competent, admired, and emotionally articulate enough to perform decency convincingly.

This does not mean kindness is fake. It means kindness is not diagnostic.

Yet women are often taught to treat respectability as a screening tool. To relax vigilance around men who "don't seem like that sort of man," without ever interrogating how flimsy that sorting system is.

Talent is not accountability.

Gentleness is not a guarantee.

Contribution is not a character reference.

When society confuses these things, women pay the price.

What Women Learn When the Story Breaks

For women reading about cases like this, the impact is rarely abstract.

Mothers revisit their assumptions about safety. Partners think back on moments of dismissed unease. Girls absorb, once again, the message that harm does not always come with warning labels.

Many women feel an additional, quieter burden: the pressure to respond correctly. To be fair. To not rush to judgment. To not appear hysterical or cynical.

But discernment is not hysteria. And withholding blind trust is not cruelty.

Women are allowed to hold complexity. To say: *I don't know what is true, but I will no longer outsource my judgment to reputation alone.*

You can respect due process without defending illusions. You can grieve the loss of an admired figure without protecting the archetype he occupied. And you can take allegations seriously without turning them into certainty.

The deeper work is internal.

It is learning to trust your own capacity to assess men without reverence. To stop confusing comfort with safety. To accept that no role, no profession, no public goodness exempts a man from scrutiny.

After the Archetype Falls

When an archetype collapses, the instinct is to replace it quickly. To find another "good man" to restore balance.

But the more radical response is to stop relying on archetypes altogether.

Men do not become trustworthy because they fit a story we like. They become trustworthy through sustained patterns of behaviour that hold up even when admiration fades and no one is watching.

This chapter is not about one man.

It is about what women are finally allowed to see when the story breaks.

And the quiet power that comes from no longer looking away.

Author's Note: *This chapter discusses a publicly reported legal case involving a well-known Australian man. The individual is not named. All references are based on contemporaneous media reporting. No findings of guilt are asserted or implied. The purpose of this chapter is cultural and psychological analysis, not legal judgment.*

Chapter 13

Men Who Can't Tell The Truth

Chronic Concealment, Emotional Immaturity, and the Cost to Women

S ome men lie occasionally.

Some men lie strategically.

And then there are men who *cannot tell the truth,* even when the truth would be easier, safer, or kinder.

This chapter is about that third category.

These are not men hiding a single mistake. They are men whose inner worlds are organised around concealment. For them, honesty is not a default—it's a threat. Truth feels destabilising, exposure feels intolerable, and accountability feels catastrophic.

Women often sense this long before they can name it. Something feels off, slippery, ungraspable. Answers never quite land. Conversations circle without resolution. And yet, because there is no single dramatic betrayal—at least not at first—women are encouraged to stay, explain, translate, and wait.

The Psychology of Chronic Concealment

Chronic concealment is not about intelligence or morality. It is about *self-protection taken to an extreme.*

For these men, the truth is experienced as:

- **Dangerous**

- **Destabilising**

- **Humiliating**

- **Identity-threatening**

So they develop a way of being in the world that prioritises *control over clarity.*

They don't necessarily plan lies in advance. More often, concealment is reflexive. Information is filtered automatically. Details are omitted without conscious deliberation. Truth is edited in real time to preserve comfort, image, and emotional equilibrium.

What women encounter is not overt dishonesty, but a persistent absence of solidity.

You ask a question – you get an answer that technically responds—but doesn't satisfy.

You follow up – you're told you're overthinking. Or worse, nagging.

And slowly, you learn that truth with this man is never complete—it is conditional.

Narcissistic, Avoidant, and Immature Patterns

Not all men who conceal chronically are narcissists. But many share overlapping traits.

Narcissistic Patterns

For men with narcissistic tendencies, truth is subordinate to self-image. What matters is not what happened, but how they are perceived.

They conceal in order to:

- **Protect superiority**

- **Avoid shame**

- **Maintain control**

- **Rewrite narratives**

Honesty is dangerous because it punctures the carefully maintained persona. When confronted, these men often respond with:

- **Minimisation**

- **Deflection**

- **Blame-shifting**

- **Gaslighting**

The goal is not resolution—it is dominance over the narrative.

Avoidant Patterns

Avoidant men are not always manipulative. Many are deeply uncomfortable with emotional exposure.

They hide because:

- **Conflict feels overwhelming.**

- **Vulnerability feels unsafe.**

- **Emotional demands feel intrusive.**

Truth requires engagement. Engagement requires presence. Avoidant men cope by disappearing emotionally while remaining physically present.

Women experience this as:

- **Evasiveness**

- **Emotional distance**

- **Chronic ambiguity**

The relationship becomes a place where nothing is openly wrong—but nothing is ever fully right.

Emotional Immaturity

Some men conceal simply because they never developed the capacity for honest self-reflection.

They lack:

- **Emotional vocabulary**

- **Accountability skills**

- **Tolerance for discomfort**

For them, truth-telling feels like punishment. They are not lying to deceive; they are lying to escape.

The problem is that women pay the price for that escape.

Trauma-Based Secrecy

Not all secrecy is malicious. Some men learned early that truth was unsafe.

Men raised in environments marked by:

- **Punishment for mistakes**

- **Emotional volatility**

- **Shame-based discipline**

- **Neglect**

- **May associate honesty with danger.**

For these men, concealment is a survival strategy that never evolved.

But survival strategies that once protected a child can devastate an adult relationship.

Trauma explains secrecy—it does not excuse its impact.

A man's unhealed past does not entitle him to withhold reality from the woman sharing his present.

How Women Get Trapped in the Pattern

Women often respond to chronic concealment by becoming investigators, interpreters, and emotional archivists.

They:

- **Track inconsistencies.**

- **Remember details he forgets.**

- **Connect dots he refuses to see.**

- **Manage conversations around his fragility.**

Over time, women shrink. They stop asking questions. They stop trusting their instincts. They stop expecting honesty.

The relationship becomes a performance where truth is rationed and peace is conditional.

This is not intimacy. It is emotional hostage-taking.

The Line That Matters

Here is the line women are rarely encouraged to draw:

It does not matter *why* a man cannot tell the truth if the result is that you are living without clarity.

Motivation does not negate impact. Trauma does not erase consequence. Intent does not repair erosion.

A man who cannot be honest cannot be safe—emotionally, psychologically, or relationally.

What This Chapter Is Asking You to Do

Stop diagnosing him.

Stop explaining him.

Stop waiting for the version of him who might one day tell the truth.

Instead, ask:

Do I feel grounded or destabilised?

Do conversations lead to clarity or confusion?

Am I managing reality so he doesn't have to face it?

Honesty is not a personality trait. It is a practice. And men who refuse to practice it are not unfinished projects—they are active choices.

The truth should not have to be excavated. It should be offered.

Anything less is not complexity.

It's *concealment.*

Chapter 14

WHEN THE SECRET LIFE IS A CRIME SCENE

What the World Saw in Gisèle Pelicot

There are secrets that confuse, disturb and wound.

And then there are secrets that *reorder your understanding of reality*—the kind that do not merely alter a relationship, but expose that the relationship, as it was understood, never truly existed.

The Secrets That Obliterate Reality

The recent case of French woman Gisèle Pelicot forces us into that territory.

For fifty years, she believed she was married to a decent man. A caring man. A man who, by all outward appearances, lived an ordinary, even loving life beside her. A husband who occupied the familiar category women are encouraged to trust: stable, present, unremarkable in the most reassuring way.

Nothing about that life suggested danger. Nothing signalled that the man beside her was living another existence entirely—one that did not merely run parallel to hers, but depended on her complete unawareness.

The Rupture

When the truth emerged, it did not arrive as a misunderstanding or a betrayal that could be contextualised.

It arrived as a rupture.

For years, her husband, Dominique Pelicot, had been living an entirely separate existence—one constructed not from quiet omissions or emotional evasions, but from something far darker.

He had been orchestrating a sustained pattern of abuse: drugging her into unconsciousness and facilitating her repeated violation by scores of other men.

While she slept. Comatose, unaware, unable to consent.

This was not a single act, not a moment of failure or moral collapse, but a system. A hidden life structured around extreme gaslighting, control, secrecy, and the absolute certainty that she would not know.

Let that sit.

Because this is the point where many people instinctively retreat into disbelief—not just at the crime, but at the *possibility* of such complete concealment.

It is almost impossible to absorb this without instinctively searching for signs—some missed signal, some overlooked clue that might make the story feel less incomprehensible.

The reflex is immediate and deeply ingrained: *How could she not have known?*

The question is framed as curiosity and asked with disbelief, and most often, judgement.

But this question reveals more about society than it does about the woman. It carries a quiet insistence that awareness should have been possible, that vigilance should have prevented this, that women bear some responsibility for detecting the undetectable.

It reveals the enduring myths that: dangerous men are obvious and that harm always announces itself.

This book has already dismantled that myth.

Men do not need to appear monstrous to do harm. They need only to be believed.

And belief is something women are trained to hold—especially in men who appear calm, stable, and "good."

The Lie That Protects Men

This is the lie that protects male secrecy at every level.

Because what this case exposes, with brutal clarity, is that *harm does not always announce itself.*

It does not always look like danger. It does not always disrupt the surface of daily life.

A man can be polite, consistent, outwardly calm, and still maintain a hidden world that is not merely separate, but fundamentally incompatible with the reality he presents. The assumption that women can always "sense" danger is comforting, but it is also false—and it shifts responsibility away from the person who constructed the deception.

The Ultimate Hidden Room

In earlier chapters, we explored the hidden rooms men maintain. The emotional ones. The psychological ones. The behavioral ones. We have examined the smaller forms of concealment: omissions, evasions, emotional withdrawal, carefully managed truths.

Those patterns matter not because they are equivalent to what happened here, but because they share a common foundation—the permission granted to men to divide themselves into compartments, and the expectation placed on women to accept what they are shown as sufficient.

This case forces us to confront the most extreme version: A hidden life that operates in direct opposition to the visible one. A man who could share a home, share a bed, share a family, share a life, while simultaneously constructing a reality his partner was never permitted to see.

This is not about complexity - it is *compartmentalization taken to its most terrifying conclusion.*

In this case, that division was absolute. One life was visible, legible, and socially validated. The other was hidden, methodical, and sustained over years.

The distance between those two realities is what makes the truth so destabilising. It forces a recognition that the "good man" and the dangerous one are not always distinguishable by surface behaviour alone.

The Secondary Injury

When the truth came to light, another pattern emerged—one that follows women even in the aftermath of extreme harm.

Attention shifted, however briefly, toward her perception.

Questions surfaced about awareness, about signs, about what might have been noticed.

This is the secondary injury: not only the harm itself, but the cultural instinct to examine the woman's knowledge rather than the man's actions. To locate the failure in her, not him.

This is the secondary violence that women experience in the wake of male deception.

And this is precisely what Gisèle Pelicot refused.

The Shame is Not Hers to Carry

What makes Gisèle Pelicot extraordinary is not only what she endured, but that she waived her anonymity.

She chose to be seen.

Not because she had something to prove—but because she understood something fundamental: *The shame did not – and should not – belong to her. It belonged to her abusers.*

By refusing to carry shame that was never hers, she disrupted a pattern that is deeply embedded: that women must absorb the consequences of male secrecy quietly, privately, and without disrupting the social order that allowed it.

As well as shame, she refused silence. And she refused to protect the man who had hidden behind her life.

Her decision was not symbolic. It was corrective.

Because shame is one of the mechanisms that allows secrecy to persist.

If women can be made to feel responsible—for trusting, for not seeing, for being associated—then the focus shifts away from the structures that enable concealment.

By placing the shame where it belongs, she altered the narrative. Not entirely, not permanently—but enough to expose the imbalance.

The Continuum of Secrecy

It is important to say this clearly: this case is extreme. It is not representative of most relationships, nor should it be used to suggest that all men are capable of such acts.

But it is not disconnected from the patterns explored throughout this book. It is the far edge of the same continuum—the point at which concealment, entitlement, and lack of scrutiny converge without interruption.

At one end of that continuum are the quiet evasions women are taught to overlook. At the other is something like this: a hidden life so complete that it renders the visible one almost irrelevant.

What connects them is not scale, but structure. The ability to hide. The expectation of being believed. The absence of meaningful challenge.

The Final Illusion

This chapter is not here to shock for its own sake. It is here to remove the last refuge of denial—the idea that secrecy is inherently limited, that there are natural boundaries men do not cross, that the surface of a life reliably reflects what lies beneath it.

You cannot always know what a man is hiding.

No amount of vigilance guarantees protection from something deliberately concealed. But the inability to know is not a failure of perception, and it is not a moral shortcoming.

The responsibility for secrecy lies with the one who keeps it. Not the one who trusted.

And the most dangerous extension of secrecy is not the hidden act itself, but the belief that someone else should have seen it coming.

Chapter 15

After the Unthinkable

Returning to Ground

After a chapter like the last, there is a natural instinct to pull back—to reassure yourself that what you've just read is distant, exceptional, unlikely to intersect with your own life.

And in many ways, that instinct is correct.

What happened to Gisèle Pelicot sits at the far edge of human behaviour. It is not the norm. It is not representative of most men, most relationships, or most lives.

It is extreme in both scale and cruelty.

But dismissing it entirely—as something separate, unrelated, irrelevant—is its own kind of mistake.

Because the purpose of that story was never to suggest that all men are dangerous. It was to dismantle a more subtle, more persistent illusion: that *we can always tell who is safe by how they appear.*

Getting Back to Reality

Most relationships do not contain crimes.

Most men are not living lives that dark.

But many relationships *do* contain:

- **Silence that goes unexplained.**

- **Truths that are delayed.**

- **Emotions that are avoided.**

- **Details that are withheld.**

- **Realities that are softened, edited, or rearranged.**

These are not the same as what you've just read. But they exist on the same spectrum.

And the danger is not in confusing the two. The danger is in **ignoring the connection between them entirely**.

What This Book Is—and Is Not—Saying

This book is not asking you to become fearful.

It is not asking you to assume the worst.

It is not asking you to see danger where there is none.

It is asking something far more grounded: To *stop outsourcing your perception.*

To recognise that clarity matters more than comfort, patterns matter more than promises, and behaviour matters more than image.

And most importantly, that not knowing everything does not make you naïve—but ignoring what you *do* know will cost you.

The Return to Yourself

After confronting the outer limits of secrecy, this work now becomes quieter.

It is no longer about extreme cases.

It is about your own experience: What you have noticed. What you have questioned. What you have explained away. What you have felt, even when you could not name it.

This is where discernment begins—not in fear, but in attention.

Moving Forward Without Fear

You do not need to become suspicious to be aware.

You do not need to harden yourself to be protected.

You do not need to assume the worst to refuse illusion.

The goal is not vigilance as anxiety.

It is awareness as steadiness.

To be present enough to see what is there. And grounded enough not to distort it.

The Line That Matters

There will always be things you cannot know. That is part of being human, part of loving anyone.

But there is a difference between what is unknowable and what is visible but unacknowledged

This book is about that difference.

Closing

Part IV has taken you to the edge—where secrecy becomes dangerous, where concealment becomes harm, where illusion collapses.

What comes next is not more exposure.

It is *protection.*

Not through fear. Not through control. But through clarity, boundaries, and the quiet, radical act of trusting what you see.

Because once you understand how secrecy works, you no longer have to live inside it.

Chapter 16

The Architecture of Silence

Power, Secrecy, and What the Epstein Files Reveal

By now we understand that:

- Male secrecy is not random.
- It exists on a spectrum.
- It is reinforced socially.

From the Unthinkable to the Unseen

If the previous chapters revealed the most intimate and devastating form of hidden harm, they also leave behind a quieter, more unsettling question: What allows secrecy to endure for so long, sometimes in plain sight?

Not every hidden life exists in isolation. Some are sustained by something broader—by status, by deference, by systems that discourage scrutiny and reward silence.

When secrecy moves beyond the private and into the protected, it changes shape. It becomes less about what one man hides, and more about what others choose not to see.

The next chapter shifts the lens outward—from the hidden rooms of individual men to the structures that allow those rooms, in certain circumstances, to remain firmly closed.

There are secrets kept within relationships. There are secrets kept within families.

And then there are secrets that appear to sit *above ordinary life entirely*—protected not just by individuals, but by networks, institutions, and silence that stretches far beyond one man.

The case of Jeffrey Epstein occupies that space.

It is not included here to catalogue allegations or rehearse details. Those have been widely reported, examined, and contested across jurisdictions and media. What matters for this book is something more structural, and more unsettling:

What happens when secrecy is no longer personal—but systemic?

When Secrecy Scales Up

Most of this book has focused on the hidden lives of individual men—their omissions, evasions, compartmentalisation, and private worlds.

The Epstein Files exposé expands that frame.

Here, secrecy was not simply about one man concealing behaviour from a partner. It existed within a broader environment of:

- **Wealth.**

- **Access.**

- **Influence.**

- **Institutional proximity.**

In such environments, secrecy does not rely on silence alone. It is reinforced by:

- **Reputation.**

- **Social standing.**

- **Perceived credibility.**

- **The reluctance of others to question what appears established and legitimate.**

This is where secrecy changes form. It becomes less about hiding—and more about *not being challenged.*

The Power of Reputation

One of the most persistent beliefs in society is that character can be inferred from status.

If a man is successful, well-connected, socially accepted and moves comfortably in respected circles, then he is often granted a presumption of legitimacy that goes largely unexamined.

This is not naivety. It is conditioning.

Reputation functions as a kind of protective layer. It does not prove innocence, but it discourages scrutiny. It makes doubt feel inappropriate, even disloyal. It shifts the burden of proof onto those who question, rather than those who act.

In environments where reputation is strong, secrecy does not need to be air-tight. It only needs to be *inconvenient to confront.*

The Silence Around Power

Large-scale secrecy rarely survives through one person alone.

It is sustained through:

- **People who look away.**

- **Systems that move slowly or selectively.**

- **Social dynamics that discourage disruption.**

- **The human tendency to defer to authority.**

This does not require coordination in the dramatic sense. It often emerges through smaller, quieter choices: not asking, not pushing, not wanting to know.

And over time, those choices accumulate into something that looks like protection.

Why This Matters to Women

It is important to say clearly: most women will never encounter anything resembling the scale or context of this case.

But the underlying dynamics are not foreign.

The same patterns exist—on a smaller, more intimate level—in everyday life:

- **The assumption that a man's outward stability reflects his inner reality.**

- **The reluctance to question what appears socially validated.**

- **The tendency to override intuition in the presence of confidence or status.**

The difference is not kind. It is scale.

The Limits of Knowing

Cases like this often produce a particular kind of unease.

Not only because of what is reported, but because of what remains unclear, disputed, or incomplete.

The public conversation becomes filled with fragments—documents, testimonies, denials, interpretations—without a single, stable narrative.

This uncertainty can be uncomfortable. It resists closure. It leaves space for speculation, but also for restraint.

And that restraint matters.

This book does not ask you to draw conclusions about individuals you do not know. It asks you to recognise patterns that are already visible.

The Pinnacle of Secrecy

If earlier chapters explored hidden rooms, and later ones exposed hidden lives, this case represents something else again: *An architecture of secrecy that extends beyond the individual.*

A structure where:

- **Visibility coexists with concealment.**

- **Influence reduces scrutiny.**

- **Truth, even when partially revealed, struggles to settle.**

It is not necessary to resolve every detail to understand what it shows.

That secrecy, when supported by power, becomes harder to see—not because it is invisible, but because it is *protected from ordinary questioning.*

Bringing It Back to Clarity

This chapter is not here to create suspicion about the world at large.

It is here to reinforce a quieter, more practical truth: You do not need access to global networks of power to understand how secrecy works.

You only need to recognise that:

- **Appearance is not evidence.**

- **Reputation is not transparency.**

- **Confidence is not clarity.**

At every level—personal or systemic—secrecy depends on the same conditions: Being believed. Not being questioned. And operating just beyond the reach of scrutiny.

Once you see that, the scale becomes less important.

Because the pattern is the same.

This is not just about 'bad men'. This is about *how secrecy survives.*

PART V – HOW WOMAN CAN PROTECT THEMSELVES

Chapter 17

Boundaries that Reveal Truth

Demanding Honesty and Reclaiming Your Energy

Before we dive into strategies, let's get something straight: *Feminism is not a war on men.*

It is not about angry, hairy-legged lesbians plotting to take over the planet (although if that scenario exists, more power to them).

Feminism is simple: it is about respect, equality, and refusing to tolerate bullshit.

It is about claiming the right to clarity, honesty, and dignity in every relationship, without excusing evasions or hiding behind excuses.

When you hear the word "feminist," I want you to hear it as a battle cry *for your own self-respect*, not a manifesto against men.

The tools, strategies, and fury in this chapter are not designed to punish men—they are designed to stop you from being punished by them.

Protecting your energy, demanding transparency, and refusing to absorb labor that isn't yours is not anti-men.

It is *pro-you.*

Strategies for Handling Male Secrecy

Here are practical (and not at all radical) feminist strategies to help you navigate male secrecy, set boundaries and reclaim energy:

1. See Clearly Before You Engage

Red flags and patterns matter. Make note of them. Do not ignore them, rationalize them, or assume they'll disappear.

Keep a mental—or literal—record of evasions, inconsistencies, and omissions.

Track repeated behaviors, not just isolated incidents.

Name what you notice: *"He avoids this topic, consistently."*

Clarity is your weapon. Once you see patterns, you can act strategically.

2. Ask Direct Questions—And Insist on Answers

Evasion thrives on ambiguity. The solution is blunt honesty:

Ask what you need to know.

Do not soften your language unnecessarily.

Insist on clarity without apology.

Examples:

"I need to know about your past relationship with X. I am not asking to punish, I am asking to understand."

"When you avoid discussing your mistakes, it affects my trust. Can you be transparent?"

If he retreats, deflects, or gets defensive, do not let excuses obscure the red flags.

3. Set Boundaries Ruthlessly

Boundaries are feminist armor. They are not negotiable, and they are not optional.

Decide what you will and will not tolerate.

Communicate boundaries clearly, without justification.

Enforce boundaries consistently.

Examples:
"If you continue to hide significant details, I cannot engage in this conversation."

"I will not manage your guilt or secrets. That labor is yours, not mine."

Boundaries are not punishment—they are self-preservation.

4. Stop Excusing, Rationalizing, or Absorbing Labor

Every time you excuse, you reinforce the pattern. Every time you absorb the fallout, you maintain the status quo.

Refuse to rationalize omissions: *"He didn't tell me because..."*

Refuse to explain inconsistencies to yourself: *"It must have been nothing."*

Trust your instincts and don' allow yourself to be gaslit. *"Perhaps it's all in my head."* No, it probably isn't.

Refuse to smooth over evasions for his comfort.

Your energy is finite. Stop giving it to secrecy.

5. Reclaim Your Emotional Energy

Male secrecy thrives on borrowed labor. The antidote is ownership of your own emotional space:

Protect your time and attention.

Prioritize your emotional health over his comfort.

Refuse to absorb guilt for his omissions or evasions.

This is radical. It is feminist. It is liberating.

6. Decide Your Engagement—And Stick to It

Once you see, name, and protect, you have options:

i) Confront and Demand Transparency
If he respects boundaries and provides clarity, continue—but do not forget red flags.

ii) Step Back or Disengage
If he refuses honesty or evades accountability, remove yourself from the cycle of secrecy.

iii) Walk Away Without Guilt

Your clarity, trust, and energy are not negotiable.

Exiting is not failure.

It is an act of respecting and reclaiming yourself.

7. The Feminist Mindset

The ultimate strategy is mindset. *This is not radical feminism.*

- **Clarity is power.**

- **Boundaries are non-negotiable.**

- **Excusing secrecy is complicity.**

- **Your energy is yours.**

You do not need permission to demand honesty.

You do not need validation to protect your trust.

You do not need to explain yourself for wanting transparency.

The moment you embrace these truths, male secrecy loses its control.

Takeaway Toolkit
- **See clearly.**

- **Name patterns.**

- **Insist on honesty.**

- **Set boundaries.**

- **Stop absorbing labor.**

- **Reclaim your energy.**

- **Choose engagement wisely.**

It is not easy. It is not polite. It is not what society has trained you to do.

It is feminist, furious, and *necessary*.

Chapter 18

The Art of Questioning Men

What to Ask, When to Ask, and How to Ask

There is a quiet skill women are rarely taught: how to ask questions that protect them without apologising for wanting the truth.

Women are often told that asking questions is intrusive, unromantic, or "too much." That curiosity ruins the mood. That trust means silence. That if something is meant to be, it will simply reveal itself in time.

This brief chapter exists to undo these fallacies.

Asking the right questions is not interrogation. It is discernment. It is how women gather information without surrendering dignity, intuition, or emotional safety.

What, When, and How to Ask
Not all questions are created equal—and timing matters.

What to Ask
Early questions should not be designed to extract confessions. They should be designed to *observe how a man relates to truth.*

Pay attention to:

- **How easily he reflects.**

- **Whether he becomes defensive.**

- **Whether he can tolerate or how he handles discomfort.**

- **Whether he speaks with ownership or deflection.**

You are not listening for perfection. You are listening for *pattern*.

When to Ask

The best time to ask meaningful questions is *before* emotional investment is high.

Once attachment deepens, women begin to negotiate against their own interests. We soften. We delay. We excuse. We tell ourselves it's "not the right moment."

In reality, clarity feels safest early—before we have something to lose.

How to Ask

Ask calmly. Ask plainly. Ask *once*.

Avoid:

- **Apologising for curiosity.**

- **Over-explaining why you're asking.**

- **Cushioning questions to manage his reaction.**

A man who reacts poorly to respectful curiosity is not revealing sensitivity—he is revealing *fragility*.

Questions Revealing Values vs Facts

Facts tell you what happened.

Values tell you *who he is when things go wrong.*

Fact-Based Questions

These are concrete and useful:

"How did your last relationship end?"

"Have you ever lived with a partner?"

"What happened with your previous job?"

But facts can be curated.

Values-Based Questions

These are harder to fake:

"What do you think you contributed to your last breakup?"

"What's something you had to take responsibility for later in life?"

"How do you usually respond when someone is disappointed in you?"

"What do you do when you realise you've hurt someone?"

Values-based questions reveal:

- **Accountability.**

- **Emotional maturity.**

- **Capacity for reflection.**

- **Relationship to shame.**

Watch whether he answers thoughtfully—or pivots, jokes, minimises, or reframes himself as the victim.

Why Women Skip the Deeper Questions

Women often skip the deeper questions in early relationships.

We don't avoid deep questions because we don't care.

We avoid them because they have been taught to prioritise *male comfort over female clarity.*

Women skip questions because:

- **They don't want to seem demanding.**

- **They fear being labelled suspicious or insecure.**

- **They've been told love requires trust before evidence.**

- **They hope time will answer what conversation won't**

Fearing the Truth

There is also a darker reason:

Women are often afraid of what they'll hear.

We don't want to jeopardise the relationship, i.e. "Scare him off", after investing in it.

Our pride doesn't want the relationship to fail.

We're taught to give men the benefit of the doubt.

But once you ask clearly—and receive a clear answer—you are responsible for what you know.

And knowledge removes excuses.

Chapter 19

Emotional Self-Protection Without Paranoia

Staying Intuitive, Grounded, and Dignified While Living in Reality

One of the cruelest tricks played on women is the false choice between two positions: *trusting blindly* and *becoming paranoid*.

As if emotional self-protection inevitably turns a woman into someone suspicious, brittle, or joyless. As if paying attention is the same thing as assuming the worst.

It isn't.

This chapter is about a third position—one women are rarely taught but desperately need: *calm vigilance without fear,* intuition without obsession, clarity without cruelty.

Emotional self-protection that does not harden you, hollow you out, or turn love into surveillance.

Discernment is not distrust. Curiosity is not cynicism. Vigilance is not anxiety.

The goal is *not* to catch men out. The goal is to *stay oriented to reality*.

Intuition Without Suspicion

Suspicion hunts for certainty to soothe fear. If you feel frantic, hyper-vigilant, or obsessed with finding proof, pause. Anxiety clouds judgement.

If you feel calm, observant, grounded—trust what you're noticing.

Intuition is quiet, embodied, and patient. It notices patterns without panic. It does not demand immediate answers.

It shows up as:

- **A subtle sense of misalignment.**

- **A feeling that something isn't landing.**

- **A repeated moment of confusion that doesn't resolve.**

Suspicion, by contrast, is loud. It is future-focused and anxious. It scans for danger because it fears being hurt again. It looks for proof in order to feel safe.

The key difference is *urgency.*

Intuition says: *"Something here deserves attention."*

Suspicion says: *"I must resolve this now or I won't be okay."*

When women have been gaslit, dismissed, or betrayed in the past, suspicion can masquerade as intuition. The work is not to silence yourself, but to slow down.

You do not need *certainty* to stay oriented.

You need *awareness.*

The Difference Between Vigilance and Anxiety

Vigilance is grounded in the present.

It says:

- **"I'm paying attention."**

- **"I'm gathering information."**

- **"I don't need answers immediately."**

Vigilance is:

- **Noticing patterns over time.**

- **Observing how words and behavior align.**

- **Allowing information to accumulate.**

- **Staying curious rather than reactive.**

Anxiety is hijacked by the future. It screams:

- **"I need certainty now."**

- **"I'm afraid of being wrong."**

- **I must resolve this feeling."**

Anxiety is:

- **Replaying conversations.**

- **Searching for hidden meanings.**

- **Needing reassurance to regulate emotion.**

- **Mistaking urgency for insight.**

Vigilance creates space.

Anxiety collapses it.

Healthy self-protection needs space, not urgency.

Women are often told they are "overthinking" when they are actually being vigilant in an environment that has not earned their trust. The goal is not to eliminate vigilance—it is to remove fear from it.

You are allowed to pay attention without being afraid.

Maintaining Dignity While Gathering Truth

Dignity is the difference between discernment and self-betrayal.

Gathering truth with dignity means:
- **Not sacrificing self-respect for reassurance.**

- **Not begging for honesty.**

- **Asking clear questions without apology.**

- **Observing responses without chasing conversations or explanations.**

- **Letting silence speak when words don't come.**

- **Accepting answers as information, not invitations to argue.**

Dignity does *not* mean:

- **Interrogating**

- **Monitoring**

- **Proving**

- **Persuading someone to be honest.**

You cannot extract truth from someone who is committed to concealment. All you can do is notice whether truth is offered freely or rationed reluctantly.

A woman maintaining dignity does not need to catch a man out. She simply watches how he handles openness and *listens to how he responds when truth is invited.*

Does he:

- **Engage or evade?**

- **Reflect or deflect?**

- **Take ownership or reposition himself as the victim?**

The answers arrive without force.

Why Women Abandon Dignity First

When emotional stakes rise, women are taught to sacrifice dignity in the name of love.

We chase clarity.

We over-explain.

We soften boundaries.

We ask the same question five different ways, hoping for a different answer.

This is not because women are weak. It's because women are *relationally* trained to preserve connection at personal cost.

Emotional self-protection means recognising the moment when *seeking reassurance* turns into *self-erasure*.

The moment you feel smaller for asking a reasonable question is the moment dignity is already being traded away.

Trust Is Not Blindness

Trust is not the absence of questions.
It is the presence of consistent, earned answers.

You do not stay open by closing your eyes.

You stay open by staying *awake*.

A woman who protects herself emotionally:

- Does not rush intimacy.

- Does not explain away discomfort.

- Does not confuse calm with safety.

- Does not hand over trust before it is earned.

She allows relationships to reveal themselves over time.

The Quiet Strength of Grounded Women

When women stop treating questions as risks, something changes.

Men who are capable of honesty lean in. Men who rely on concealment become uncomfortable.

Both outcomes are useful

The art of asking the right questions is not about controlling the future. It is about *protecting your present*—your clarity, your time, your emotional energy.

A grounded woman is not suspicious. She is not cynical. She is not hardened.

She is simply no longer willing to abandon herself in order to maintain peace.

She understands that:

- **Intuition doesn't need proof.**

- **Clarity doesn't need conflict.**

- **Truth doesn't need force.**

She watches. She listens. She asks when it matters. And she accepts what is revealed—without bargaining with reality.

That is emotional self-protection without paranoia.

Not fear-based.

Not defensive.

Just awake, dignified, and unwilling to disappear.

That is R.E.S.P.E.C.T.

Self-respect.

PART VI – WHEN TRUTH HEALS

Chapter 20

The Confession Window

When Truth Emerges, and What Makes It Possible

There is a moment in many relationships that arrives quietly and leaves quickly.

A narrowing of time. A softening of defences. A sudden willingness to speak.

This is the *confession window*.

It is not planned. It is not promised. And it does not stay open for long.

When it appears, it offers a rare glimpse into a man's inner world—what he has hidden, what he fears, and what he is finally ready to risk losing in order to be known.

Understanding this window matters, because when it is mishandled, it slams shut. Sometimes forever.

Why Men Open Up Suddenly

Men rarely confess in stages.

They hold, compartmentalize, suppress—and then release.

This is not because men are more deceptive by nature, but because many are emotionally trained to treat disclosure as dangerous.

Truth, to them, often feels like an irreversible act: once spoken, it cannot be unsaid, forgiven, or controlled.

Men tend to open up suddenly for a few key reasons:

- **Internal pressure reaches saturation**

Guilt, cognitive dissonance, or the exhaustion of maintaining a false self becomes unbearable.

- **A threat to the relationship becomes real**

Distance, withdrawal, or the genuine possibility of loss can rupture denial.

- **A moment of unexpected safety appears**

Not interrogation, but calm presence. Not accusation, but steadiness.

- **A developmental shift occurs**

Age, illness, fatherhood, therapy, or a crisis can loosen long-held defences.

Confession often comes not when a man feels brave—but when he can no longer tolerate the cost of silence.

How to Recognize When He Wants to Tell the Truth

Before truth is spoken, it is often *telegraphed*.

Men on the edge of confession frequently display subtle but consistent signs:

- **He becomes unusually reflective or subdued.**

- **He circles a topic without naming it.**

- **He asks hypothetical questions about forgiveness, endings, or "what you'd do if…".**

- **He shows restlessness, irritability, or emotional fatigue.**

- **He tests safety with partial truths or minimized disclosures.**

This is not manipulation. It is rehearsal.

Many men need to sense the emotional weather before stepping fully into honesty. They are checking: *Will I survive this? Will you?*

The confession window is not opened by pressure. It opens when a man feels both *seen and uncornered.*

What Encourages Honesty

Honesty is not encouraged by moral superiority, emotional volatility, or the promise of immediate forgiveness.

It is encouraged by *containment.*

What helps truth emerge:

- **Emotional regulation**

Calm does not mean approval. It means capacity.

- **Clear boundaries**

"I want the truth" is more powerful than "I need reassurance."

- **Fewer words, more presence**

Silence often invites more honesty than questioning.

- **No premature bargaining**

Promising outcomes before hearing the truth collapses trust.

- **Respect for the moment**

Treating disclosure as significant, not inconvenient or theatrical.

Paradoxically, honesty flourishes when it is not demanded, but *allowed*.

What Closes the Window

Just as important as what opens the confession window is what closes it.

The window shuts when:

- **Disclosure is met with ridicule or contempt.**

- **The woman immediately centres her own fear or rage.**

- **The truth is used instantly as leverage.**

- **The man is punished for honesty rather than held accountable.**

This does not mean women must absorb harm quietly. It means timing matters.

Truth needs air before it can be reckoned with.

When Truth Heals—and When It Doesn't

Not all confessions lead to repair. Some reveal incompatibility, danger, or deception too deep to bridge.

Healing does not mean staying.

It means reality replacing confusion.

A confession that heals:

- **Restores coherence.**

- **Ends self-doubt.**

- **Clarifies choices.**

- **Returns a woman to her own intuition.**

Even when the truth hurts, it can be a form of relief.

Pain with clarity is less corrosive than comfort built on illusion.

The Courage to Receive the Truth

The confession window asks something of women too. Not endless patience. Not instant forgiveness. Not emotional sacrifice.

It asks for steadiness. The ability to listen without collapsing. To hear without rewriting. To allow truth to land before deciding what it means.

When truth heals, it is not because it saves the relationship. It heals because it *ends the lie.*

And sometimes, that is the beginning—not of togetherness—but of *freedom.*

Chapter 21

HELPING A MAN CONFRONT HIS SECRETS

Gentle Truth, Without Self-Betrayal

There is a difference between extracting a confession and inviting reckoning.

Many women, once sensing something hidden, feel torn between two instincts: the urge to confront and the fear of becoming accusatory, nagging, or unsafe.

So they soften, wait, rationalize.

Or they explode.

Neither approach helps a man face his secrets. One enables avoidance; the other entrenches it.

Helping a man confront his secrets is not about managing him into honesty. It is about creating conditions where truth becomes the least frightening option available.

Gentle Confrontation: Firm Without Force

Gentle confrontation is often misunderstood as passivity. It is not.

It is clarity without cruelty.

Gentle confrontation looks like:

- Naming what you observe, not what you assume

- Speaking in present reality, not historical indictments

- Refusing minimisation without escalating threat

"I notice you shut down whenever this comes up."

"I sense there's something unresolved here."

"I'm not accusing you—but I'm not ignoring this either."

This approach removes the usual escape routes. He cannot argue with hysteria, because there is none. He cannot dismiss it as imagination, because it is grounded in observable behavior.

Gentle confrontation communicates something powerful: *I see you clearly, and I am steady enough to stay present.*

That steadiness often destabilizes secrecy more than anger ever could.

Separating Accountability from Annihilation

Shame is secrecy's greatest ally.

Many men hide not because they are malicious, but because they equate exposure with total collapse: loss of respect, loss of identity, loss of worth.

When shame floods the nervous system, honesty feels existentially dangerous.

Conversations must endeavor to be shame-free. But shame-free does *not* mean consequence-free.

It means:

- **Distinguishing behavior from identity.**

- **Holding accountability without moral annihilation.**

- **Refusing to humiliate in order to feel powerful.**

"You're not a monster—but this matters."

"This behavior has consequences, and we need to talk about them."

"I can be disappointed without destroying you."

When a man feels that truth will not erase his humanity, he is more likely to risk it.

Women are often taught that expressing disappointment is cruelty. It isn't. Contempt is cruelty. Calm disappointment is clarity.

Inviting Growth Instead of Defensiveness

Defensiveness is not proof of guilt—it's proof of feeling threatened.

When men feel cornered, they revert to familiar strategies: deflection, minimisation, anger, intellectualisation, silence. These are not conscious tactics; they are protective reflexes.

Growth is invited when:

- **The focus shifts from "why did you do this?" to "what's going on** inside you?"

- **The conversation allows space for reflection, not just response.**

- **Curiosity replaces cross-examination.**

"What do you think this pattern costs you?"

"When did you first learn to hide like this?"

"What would change if you didn't have to keep this secret anymore?"

These questions do not excuse harm. They re-orient the conversation toward responsibility rather than self-defence.

Importantly, inviting growth does not mean waiting indefinitely. An invitation has a shelf life.

The Boundary Women Must Hold

Helping a man confront his secrets is not a duty. It is a choice.

Women are not rehabilitation centres for emotionally underdeveloped men. Nor are they required to make themselves smaller, quieter, or safer than they already are.

A crucial boundary:
- **You can create conditions for truth, but...**

- **You cannot force maturity.**

- **You must not sacrifice your own dignity to manage his fear.**

Sometimes a man will rise to the invitation. Sometimes he will retreat deeper into denial.

His response tells you everything you need to know.

When Helping Becomes Harmful

There is a line where patience turns into self-abandonment.

Helping becomes harmful when:

- **You do all the emotional labor.**

- **You repeatedly absorb his discomfort.**

- **You wait for insight that never arrives.**

- **You silence your intuition in order to protect his ego.**

Growth requires participation. If he will not step forward, no amount of gentleness will pull him there.

Truth as an Offering, Not a Demand

The most effective stance is neither force nor fragility.

It is this:

"I am open to truth. I am capable of hearing it. And I will not build my life around what remains hidden."

This posture does something remarkable. It removes the power struggle. It centres reality. It makes honesty a choice—not a concession.

When a man confronts his secrets under these conditions, it is not because he was dragged there.

It is because, for the first time, *the cost of hiding outweighed the risk of being seen.*

Chapter 22

Rebuilding Trust

After Hidden Things Surface

Truth does not automatically heal. Sometimes it simply arrives.

When hidden things surface, many women feel immediate pressure to be *reasonable, fair, understanding*.

There is an unspoken expectation that once the secret is out, forgiveness should follow quickly, neatly, and quietly.

But trust is not restored by disclosure alone.

In fact, disclosure is only the beginning.

Rebuilding trust is not about saving the relationship at all costs. It is about discovering whether the relationship can exist *without costing you yourself.*

Repairing Without Self-Betrayal

Repair is often framed as something women must *do*: process, forgive, soothe, stabilise. This framing is dangerous.

Repair without self-betrayal means:

- **You do not rush clarity for the sake of peace**

- **You do not minimise harm to appear magnanimous**

- **You do not carry his guilt, shame, or recovery**

True repair centres *impact*, not intent.

"I'm not deciding anything yet."

"I need time to see consistency, not promises."

"I will not pretend this didn't change how I see you."

These are not punishments. They are boundaries.

If honesty now requires you to silence your anger, grief, or confusion, the repair is already false.

When to Stay and When to Go

Staying is not a moral virtue. It is a practical and emotional decision.

Leaving is often framed as failure. It isn't.

When Staying Is Worth Considering

Staying may be worth considering if:

- **He takes responsibility without defensiveness.**

- **He does not pressure you to "move on".**

- **He tolerates your questions without resentment.**

- **His behaviour changes *before* forgiveness is offered.**

- **Most importantly: He accepts that rebuilding trust is *his* work, not yours.**

You are not staying because he is devastated. You are staying because his actions show accountability over time.

When Leaving Is the Healthiest Choice

Leaving is appropriate when:

- **He minimises or reframes the harm.**

- **He becomes impatient with your healing.**

- **He wants credit for honesty but resists change.**

- **The truth keeps coming in instalments.**

- **You feel smaller, quieter, or less intuitive than before.**

If the relationship requires you to doubt your own perception in order to continue, the cost is too high. Trust cannot be rebuilt in an environment where truth is rationed.

How to Know If Real Change Is Happening

Words are cheap after exposure. Behaviour is not.

Real change looks like:

- **Voluntary transparency, not forced disclosure**

- **Consistency across stress, not just calm periods**

- **Willingness to seek help without being prompted**

- **Acceptance that consequences may be permanent**

- **Most telling of all: He does not position himself as the victim of your pain.**

If you are managing his discomfort more than your own recovery, change is cosmetic.

The Question Beneath the Question

Many women ask: *Can I trust him again?*

The deeper question is: *Can I trust myself if I stay?*

Rebuilding trust is only meaningful if it restores your sense of agency, intuition, and self-respect. If staying requires emotional contortion, hypervigilance, or self-silencing, trust has not been rebuilt—it has been outsourced.

Truth Heals When It Frees

Truth heals not because it saves relationships, but because it restores reality.

Sometimes rebuilding trust means rebuilding *together*.

Sometimes it means rebuilding *alone*.

Both are valid.

Only one is honest.

The measure of healing is not whether the relationship survives.

It is whether *you* do.

PART VII – THE WOMAN WHO SEES CLEARLY

Chapter 23

The Final Act

Living With Clarity & Power – Without Excuses

T his is it.

The chapter where the excuses end. Where the rationalizations stop. Where the "good man" myth meets the hard truth: your life, your clarity, and your energy are not collateral damage for male secrecy.

If you take nothing else from this book, take this: *you do not exist to accommodate evasions, half-truths, or unprocessed shame.*

Not today. Not tomorrow. Not ever.

Step One: Own Your Clarity
Seeing patterns, recognizing red flags, demanding honesty—this is all useless unless you *claim your own clarity as sacred.*

Your intuition is not overreacting.

Your need for transparency is not nagging.

Your refusal to absorb secrets is not cruelty.

Clarity is not optional. It is your birthright.

Step Two: Stop Excusing and Absorbing

The system that rewards male secrecy relies on women excusing, smoothing, and absorbing. Refuse to play that role.

Stop rationalizing: *"It's not a big deal."*

Stop internalizing guilt for someone else's omissions.

Stop performing unpaid emotional labor that enables evasions.

When you stop excusing it, secrecy loses its power. Simple. Brutal. Necessary.

Step Three: Set Boundaries and Stick to Them

Boundaries are feminist armor. They are not negotiable, not optional, and not a favor to anyone.

Decide what you will tolerate and what you will not.

Communicate it clearly, without apology or over-explanation.

Enforce it consistently, even when it triggers resistance or drama.

A boundary is not punishment—it is self-preservation, and it is revolutionary in a world that teaches women to prioritize male comfort over their own.

Step Four: Choose Engagement Wisely

Not every secret is world-ending. Not every omission requires an exit.

But every evasive pattern must be acknowledged, addressed, and navigated strategically.

Options include:

Confront and Demand Accountability
Hold him to the truth, insist on transparency, and refuse rationalizations.

Step Back or Disengage
If he refuses to be honest, protect yourself by removing emotional labor from your life.

Walk Away Without Guilt
Ending a relationship because of secrecy is not failure—it is clarity in action.

Step Five: Embrace Your Radical Feminist Power
This is the final, furious truth:

Male secrecy is *not your problem to fix.*

Male shame is *not your burden to carry.*

Male evasions are *not your responsibility to excuse.*

Your clarity, your trust, your energy—these are non-negotiable, sacred, and yours alone. Protect them ruthlessly. Demand honesty without guilt. Refuse to manage the fallout for someone else's shame.

Step Six: Live Fully, Without Compromise
When you stop excusing, stop absorbing, and stop tolerating secrecy, something radical happens:

You regain emotional energy.

You see relationships clearly.

You navigate life without compromise for others' evasions.

You are no longer trapped in a cycle of rationalizing, excusing, and absorbing.

This is *liberation*.

This is feminism in its most uncompromising form.

If You've Made It This Far
Congratulations.

You now know what every woman eventually discovers: *men hide, even the "good" ones.*

Secrets are not anomalies—they are systemic.

Evasion is not a quirk—it is trained.

And women, for far too long, have been socialized to absorb the cost, excuse the omissions, and protect the fragile egos of men who refuse to see themselves clearly.

This ends now.

A Final Truth
Feminism is not a war on men.

It is a war on patriarchal nonsense that demands women shoulder labor that isn't theirs, rationalize evasions that cost them energy and trust, and forgive patterns that undermine their clarity.

You do not need permission to demand honesty.

You do not need validation to set boundaries.

You do not need to apologize for wanting transparency, respect, and dignity.

Your Power Is Non-Negotiable

Men's secrets cost you. Stop paying the price for someone else's shame.

Excusing evasions is complicity. Stop smoothing over what is unacceptable.

Your energy, clarity, and trust are sacred. Protect them.

Boundaries are armor. Wear them relentlessly.

Honesty is your right. Insist on it.

No compromise. No rationalizations. No excuses.

The Liberation of Seeing Clearly

When you see patterns, name red flags, and stop absorbing the fallout, something radical happens:

The hidden rooms lose their power.

Male secrecy no longer dictates your energy.

Relationships exist on your terms—or not at all.

You reclaim time, trust, and emotional space.

This is not radical only because society tries to make it so. It is radical because it is truthful, self-respecting, and unapologetic.

A Call to Action

Let this book be your manifesto. Take this knowledge and wield it like the weapon it is.

See clearly.

Name patterns.

Set boundaries.

Demand honesty.

Walk away when necessary.

Protect your energy.

Refuse to excuse secrecy.

Do not apologize for wanting clarity.

Do not apologize for expecting respect.

Do not apologize for being furious at a system that trains women to absorb what is not theirs.

Live without excuses. Live without compromise. Live with clarity, power, and fury.

And never forget: the only person whose secrets you should tolerate is yourself, and the only person you must explain your choices to is *you*.

The Final Takeaway

Women, hear this and burn it into your core:

Secrecy costs you.

Excusing it is complicity.

Your energy is finite and sacred.

Boundaries are your armor.

Honesty is non-negotiable.

Live without compromise. Live without excuses. Live with clarity, power, and fury.

Because the only secrets you should tolerate are your own, and the only person you should ever have to rationalize for is *you*.

Epilogue

The Woman Who Sees Clearly

She is not bitter. She is not hardened. She is not suspicious for the sake of it.

She is awake.

This book was never about turning women against men.

It was about turning women back toward themselves.

The woman who sees clearly does not expect perfection, confession on demand, or emotional sainthood.

She understands male psychology well enough to know *why* secrecy happens, but she no longer confuses explanation with excuse. Insight has sharpened her compassion without dulling her boundaries.

She has discernment.

Not the frantic scanning of paranoia, but the quiet pattern-recognition of someone who trusts her own perception.

She notices inconsistencies without spiralling. She hears what is said — and what is carefully avoided.

She understands that what matters is not whether a man *could* be hiding something, but whether his way of relating leaves her grounded or diminished.

She trusts herself.

This is the great recovery. She no longer gaslights her intuition in the name of being "easygoing," "fair," or "understanding."

When something feels off, she does not rush to explain it away. She sits with it. She observes. She allows time to reveal what urgency once obscured.

She has emotional boundaries.

She does not over-function for men's silence, shame, or avoidance.

She does not translate evasions, soften truths, or carry secrets that are not hers. She understands that empathy without limits becomes self-erasure — and she refuses to disappear for anyone.

She understands men more clearly than before.

Not through fantasy or denial, but through realism.

She knows how shame, entitlement, avoidance, and social reward systems shape male behaviour.

She also knows that insight does not obligate her to stay, fix, or wait. Understanding is not a contract.

And still — she can love.

This is the part the world gets wrong.

Clarity does not kill romance.

Self-trust does not destroy intimacy.

Boundaries do not prevent love.

They make it possible.

She loves without auditioning.

She connects without contorting.

She chooses without fear of being "too much" or "not enough."

And if a relationship requires blindness, self-doubt, or silence to survive — she lets it go.

Not angrily.

Not dramatically.

Just clearly.

This is the woman who no longer manages men's hidden rooms.

Who no longer mistakes secrecy for depth.

Who no longer confuses endurance with love.

She sees what is there.

She believes what she sees.

And she builds her life accordingly.

That is not cynicism.

That... is freedom.

Acknowledgments

I'd like to acknowledge the secretive men I've walked away from.
Analyzing the fallout became the unwitting inspiration for this book.

The clarity and relief were huge.
And my liberation was – and is – euphoric.

To my readers, thank you for investing in this work.
Find the strength to free yourself from men's secret lives.
Your relief will be immense as well.

Reviews Invited

The Secret Lives of Men
A Women's Guide to Male Deception, Omission and Silence

We would be grateful for your feedback.

Kindly take a moment to review the book via your bookseller's website.

The author and publisher thank you for investing your precious time in this book.

We hope you found it both reassuring and inspirational.

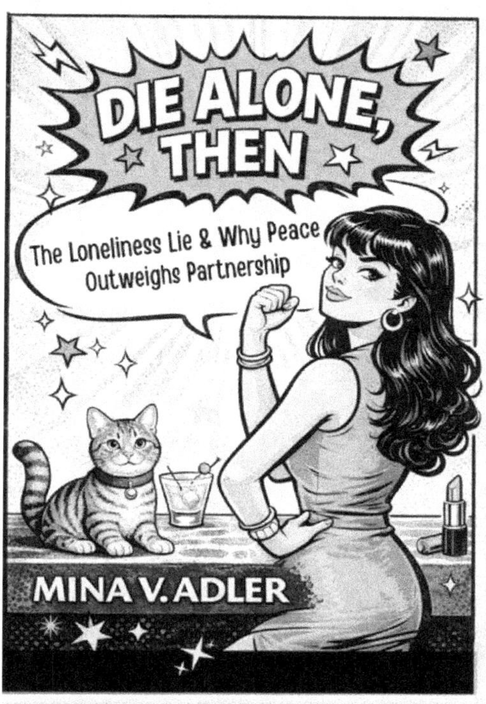

There is a threat society keeps using against women. "Lower your standards or you'll die alone!"

Women are conditioned to believe that those of us who expect too much from men or relationships – even when it isn't much at all – will end up alone.

Promises, promises. As if being alone in peace is worse than being miserable with someone.

Being alone doesn't mean being lonely. I've never felt more lonely and quietly desperate than when I was partnered with a man who disrespected and drained me.

The Pros of being alone far outweigh the Cons. The tidy home. The clean bathroom. The calm nervous systems and mental clarity. The balanced PH. The supportive friends. The conviction that You Are Enough. A peace and serenity like no other. That, to me sounds like liberation.

Society audaciously tells women to settle. To accept less. To tolerate disrespect, weaponized incompetence, emotional unavailability, and lack of effort. Just to avoid being single. That, to me, sounds more like punishment.

Men love throwing "you'll die alone" at women who have standards, but what they're really saying is: "Lower your expectations so I don't have to improve." They want access to high-value women without being high-value men. They want partnership benefits without partnership effort.

And when women refuse? They shame us with loneliness threats as if we're not watching married women be lonelier than single ones.

So yes, if having standards means being "alone" with peace, health, cleanliness, and supportive friends, women will choose that every time.

Being alone isn't the threat men think it is anymore. Being with the wrong person? That's the real nightmare.

Women better relax? No. Without unworthy men, women are finally relaxed.

You loved him. You were generous with your time, your attention, and your body. Intimacy felt natural—part of the connection you were building together.

But slowly, something changed.

Sex became reassurance. Affection became maintenance.

And the relationship you once entered with desire began to feel like something you had to manage.

The fear beneath it all: *If I don't perform, I'll be replaced.*

In The Resentment Years: When Desire Becomes Duty, Mina V. Adler explores the quiet transformation many women experience in long relationships or marriages: the moment when love turns into labor and intimacy begins to feel like obligation.

With sharp psychological insight and uncompromising honesty. Adler exposes the invisible expectations that shape modern relationships -especially the subtle pressure many women feel to maintain order and keep their man.

When did desire become duty?

Research

Case Studies & Anecdotal Experiences of Male Secrecy

Following are academic case studies, research findings, and first-person narratives which have contributed to this work about male secrecy.

Emotional Suppression & Hiding Vulnerability

According to *Psychology Today*, many men keep sexual secrets—porn use, past experiences, or cheating fantasies—because they fear their partner's judgment.

From a men's-mental-health perspective: some men fear that being emotionally vulnerable (sharing fear, sadness, or insecurity) will backfire — they worry their emotional openness could be "weaponized" against them in a relationship.

In a very honest first-person essay, psychologist Richard Nicastro wrote about how childhood trauma taught him to build a secret inner world. He admitted that because of abuse, he learned to *"wear psychological masks"*.

Emotional Suppression Being Misread / Not Spotted

A study from Washington University (reported by *ScienceDaily*) found that couples often *miss cues* when a partner is hiding their emotions. In other words, women may not spot when men are suppressing, because suppressing looks like calm or "everything's fine," even when it isn't.

This aligns with a broader psychological pattern: men are more likely to use suppression of feelings, rather than reappraisal, and partners underestimate how much suppression is going on.

Secrecy & Relationship Quality / Health Costs

Research published in *PubMed* shows that romantic secrecy (not just financial or sexual, but any kind of hidden emotional life) is linked to lower relationship quality, reduced commitment, and increased personal stress or health symptoms (anxiety, negative affect).

In a qualitative study (CSUSB ScholarWorks), researchers found that common secrets men keep include past relationships and infidelity, and that secret-keeping correlates with lower relationship satisfaction.

Financial Secrecy ("Financial Infidelity")

Financial secrecy is a very real phenomenon: "financial infidelity" includes hiding savings accounts, credit cards, or debt from a partner.

In recent surveys, many men cite shame or embarrassment about financial instability or spending as reasons not to disclose money problems to their partner.

Anecdotal / Real-Life Personal Stories (from Reddit and Online Communities)

A man on Reddit said: he suppressed his feelings for so long that even when he tried to open up, his partner reacted negatively, which reinforced his belief that vulnerability was dangerous.

Another man described how he learned to "hide my feelings" from a very young age. By age 4–6, he says he was already self-dampening, a behavior that stayed with him into adulthood.

One woman shared that after *years* of sensing something was off with her husband, he finally admitted he "usually is upset and holds it in."

Emotional Constraint & Father-Son Relationships

Anne Cleary, Frontiers in Sociology (2022) studied how emotionally distant father-son relationships teach men to suppress vulnerability. Many men in the study never learned how to express emotional distress; instead, they "sublimated problems and disguised vulnerability," leading to long-term emotional constraint and isolation.

This connects powerfully to secrecy in adult relationships: men learn early not to expose weakness, so they hide distress in romantic partnerships rather than unpack it openly.

Emotional Disclosure & Mental Health

In the study "Distress disclosure and psychological distress among men", researchers found that men who avoid sharing their emotional pain (distress concealment) are more likely to feel lonely and depressed.

Another related study ("Reduced Emotional Awareness and Distress Concealment") found that young men with poor emotional awareness hide their distress more, and this leads directly to higher loneliness.

These are not just "quirky individual cases": this is systemic — emotional concealment can be deeply harmful to men's mental health, but secrecy is often built-in by gender norms.

Secrecy and Psychological Cost

Research published in *Regulating Emotions about Secrets* shows that people (including men) use suppression, distraction, and rumination to manage the emotional burden of keeping secrets.

Crucially, even when a secret is personally harmful, people often prioritize keeping it hidden over relieving their emotional burden. This suggests that secrecy isn't just about avoidance—it's a defensive strategy, even at a cost to well-being.

Romantic Secrecy & Relationship Quality

In *Secret Romantic Relationships: Consequences for Personal and Relational Well-Being*, Justin Lehmiller's research showed that relational secrecy (hiding the very existence of a relationship) was linked to lower commitment, reduced self-esteem, and more health symptoms among partners.

Also, another study ("Are Secret Relationships Hot, Then Not?") found that secrecy can feel intense and exciting in early relationships ("obsession"), but over time it becomes burdensome and damaging.

This offers a useful metaphor for how hidden parts of a man's life may feel "romantic" or seductive at first—but the long-term costs can be profound.

Confidant's Burden: When Someone Else Hides Secrets

A study in the *Journal of Relationships Research* ("Wanna Hear a Secret?") examined how people feel when they are the confidants of someone keeping a secret. The researchers found that secret-keeping creates a cognitive burden, emotional distress, and relational distance.

Applied to romantic relationships: when a man hides things, his partner (woman) may carry invisible mental and emotional weight simply by being the one who "knows there's more" – even if she's never told everything.

Sexual Secrets & Shame

Psychologist Dr. Justin Lehmiller (again) wrote in *Psychology Today* about how many men hide aspects of their sexual lives—from pornography use to past infidelities—because of shame.

According to *Secrets and Love* (another Psychology Today article), common reasons people conceal things (sex, addiction, shame) include fear of embarrassment, self-protection, and shame about their own "undesirable" parts.

These insights align directly with your book's theme: men don't always lie to hurt—they often hide because they are deeply ashamed, and revealing would feel like a risk.

Men's Anxiety & Emotional Expression

In *"Engendered Expressions of Anxiety: Men's Emotional Communications With Women and Other Men"* (Frontiers in Sociology, 2021), researcher Brendan Gough found that men often communicate anxiety differently depending on who they're with. With other men, they may avoid showing vulnerability altogether; with women, they may still guard emotions closely because of gendered expectations around masculinity.

This supports the argument that male secrecy is not random or personal—it is socially regulated and deeply gendered.

First-Person / Anecdotal (from Online Communities)

On Reddit, one man shared how he has never opened up in a relationship because he was taught to "man up," and now thinks showing "weakness" would make women lose respect for him.

Another man wrote about feeling he has *no safe space* to express emotional pain: he said he's more comfortable sharing troubles with male friends than his partner—because women, in his experience, don't respond well when men open up emotionally.

These voices from men in real-life (or nearly real-life) online spaces highlight the emotional risk men perceive—or experience—when they attempt vulnerability.

Why This Research and These Stories Matter

These are real-world illustrations of how male secrecy isn't just about "bad guys" — even normal, decent men hide things, because of shame, cultural conditioning, or fear.

They map directly onto the core themes of this work: male compartmentalisation, the cost of emotional suppression, and the burden of unspoken labour on women.

The harm isn't just emotional: hiding emotions (or money) undermines trust, damages relationship quality, and places a hidden tax on the partner (usually women).

They reinforce the idea that secrecy is systemic, not individual: many men feel unsafe showing vulnerability, because they've been taught that emotional openness is weakness or a liability.